"A rich blend of historical ins
pondering. While you might ....g... ....ything in the book, all
of it will compel you to think more deeply about the week that changed
the world and history, the Passion of our Lord."

Abner Chou (PhD), John F. MacArthur Endowed Fellow, The Master's
University

"William Varner's book on Jesus' last week is filled with fresh insights
resulting from years of study and first-hand observation in the Holy
Land itself. Beautifully written, Passionate about the Passion Week will
make an excellent resource for laity and clergy. Scholars, too, should
read this well-informed book, for I suspect many will have to update
their lecture notes! Varner's little book is a gem and very much worth
the read. Highly recommended."

Craig A. Evans (PhD), Houston Baptist University

"Will Varner is an experienced and trusted guide both to the Bible and
to the Holy Land. I can't think of a better person to lead us through the
Scriptures and geographical details of the final days of Jesus' earthly
ministry. This volume will both educate your mind and nourish your
soul."

Robert L. Plummer (PhD), Collin and Eveyln Aikman Professor of Biblical Studies, The Southern Baptist Theological Seminary

"This unpretentious little book is full of good things. Dr. Varner set us
straight on a number of historical points, while at the same time em-
phasizing the devotional dimensions of the passion narative. In effect,
reading this book can become a spiritual exercise, especially appropriate during Passion Week but, given the central importance of these
events, useful at any time in the liturgical year."

Donald A. Hagner (PhD), George Eldon Ladd Professor Emeritus of
New Testament, Fuller Theological Seminary

"Tradition reigns during Holy Week, but with gentle prodding Will Varner pokes at what we think is true about Jesus' final week on earth and guides us into better ways of understanding. By questioning accepted interpretations and reminding us what the biblical texts actually say, this book illuminates the most important week of human history. After you rethink your assumptions and consider new ideas, you will discover that the author's passion for our Lord Jesus Christ has deepened your own."

William L. Krewson (PhD), Professor, School of Divinity, Cairn University

"This book is a masterpiece of fresh examination and insights. It is scholarly, uplifting, Christ-exalting, and God-honoring."

Dr. Gary Cohen, Retired Seminary Professor and Army Chaplain

"*Passionate about the Passion Week* has helped me read the Gospels with greater detail, looking at the complete harmony of the Passion Week. I believe it is of great value to anyone looking to preach or teach through this important part of Jesus' life and ministry."

Adam Waller, Pastor of Grace Life London

"Have you ever found yourself wondering about certain things in the Passion story that never seemed to line up with the actual biblical text? If so, you're not alone. William Varner comes to our rescue, carefully sifting through the biblical records to bring out the actual story of our Savior's passion. Buy it, read it, believe it and share it. The story is too important to miss."

Dr. David Hegg, Pastor of Grace Baptist Church, Santa Clarita, CA

Passionate about the Passion Week

A Fresh Look at Jesus' Last Days

Passionate *about the* Passion Week

A Fresh Look at Jesus' Last Days

WILLIAM VARNER

Fontes Press

Passionate about the Passion Week:
A Fresh Look at Jesus' Last Days

Copyright © 2020 by William Varner

ISBN-13: 978-1-948048-23-1 (hardback)
ISBN-13: 978-1-948048-22-4 (paperback)

Book and prayer icons at the end of each chapter are made by Freepik from www.flaticon.com.

FONTES PRESS

DALLAS, TX

www.fontespress.com

To

Douglas Bookman

Who has made a career of preaching on the Passion Week

CONTENTS

INTRODUCTION

Most of the books I have written over my career were assigned to me through an invitation to contribute to a subject or a series. A few have been written because of a desire that originated in my own heart and mind. The modest volume which is before you is one of those that I decided to write myself. I have wanted to write it for years and finally the circumstances came together to do just that. I have taught the Life of the Messiah for over thirty years and have tried to look at the events in the life of our Lord from many angles, especially paying attention to their Jewish context. The Gospel writers devote a major part of their works to what Christians call "the Passion Week." I also have given at least a third of the time in class to the events that center on those fateful last eight days, beginning with "Palm Sunday" and continuing through Resurrection Sunday, but also extending beyond the events of that week to the Ascension of our Lord forty days later.

At the end of a sabbatical, after finishing my main writing project (which was also assigned to me!), I found myself with some unexpected time on my hands, and I decided to start writing this book, simply because I am passionate about Passion Week! I mentioned some special circumstances above, and these events, unlike my sabbatical, were not planned. In May 2019 I was about to board a plane and lead my fifty first trip to Israel, the "land of our Lord." To my great shock and disappointment, I lost my passport in the airport—after I checked in! It took me nearly four days before I could get a new passport and a new flight so I could join my beloved Helen and a wonderful group of my Sojourners flock, just in time to lead them during the last week of the trip through the "last week" of Jesus in Jerusalem. I write these words on a Tuesday afternoon and I hope to get into the events of Passion week before I fly out on Friday. I know that I will not finish the book before then, but hopefully what I do write will make a good head start on the book so I can finish it during the rest of the summer.

Jesus has been the subject of more books than anyone else in history. Other authors have also written entire volumes on the events of Passion Week. Why should I be so bold to write another one? The reason is simply because I think we should look again at these familiar texts through a fresh lens! I honestly believe that I have something to say that will shed some new light on these special events. This is not because I have some special revelation or insight denied to other scholars, but because I have examined many traditional ways of reading these events and found them to be unscriptural! Some of these events have been read for so long in traditional ways that many Christians will actually be surprised when they discover that the Gospels do not say what they have heard or they say it in a different way from what they have heard. I am sorry if I step on the toes of those holding to some long-held ideas, but I do not do it to be different. First and foremost, I have tried not to be "original" but to be "Biblical" in my observations and conclusions. The reader must judge if I have been faithful to the texts rather than simply faithful to a traditional reading of the texts. After reading a rough draft of this book, my pastor, John

MacArthur, wrote to me the following. "Your insights add much to the richness of these blessed narratives. Even after all the years I have spent in the Gospels, you pulled up fresh treasures!"

A brief explanation is in order about the expression "Passion Week." Another way to describe the period is "Holy Week," while others may prefer simply "Last Week." The word "passion" is used in its older English sense, meaning "suffering," drawn from a late Latin word, *passionem*, or the Old French word, passion. Frankly, I chose the expression simply because of its similarity to the adjective "passionate" that I use in the title!

A warning is appropriate. This book will not be a treatment of each event in the Passion Week. It will focus only on the events and passages that I believe deserve a second look. But you will find that every traditional "day" in some way or another contains events that will be reexamined and freshly discussed, simply by a rereading of the Gospel texts. The book is not overly academic and can be read by anyone who has a love for the Lord and his word. My wife, Helen, who is leading that group in Israel as I write this introduction, reminds me occasionally that I need to "write a book for the rest of us." This is one of those books, which she also helped to proofread.

I want to share with you that this experience of focusing so closely on the events of those last days of Jesus has been one of the greatest spiritual disciplines that I have experienced in my over fifty years as one of his followers. My prayer is that you will also become more "passionate about Passion Week" as a result of reading these words.

Because this is not intended to be an academic style book, I have not included many citations to document my arguments, apart from the extensive Scripture references. At the end of every chapter, however, I suggest resources for further study of the subjects discussed. At the end of each chapter, I have also included a "suggested prayer" that focuses on the main themes of that chapter. In this way, I pray that the book will also serve as a devotional companion as you think through the events of Passion Week.

At a later stage in the project, my publisher suggested that we enhance the chapters with some photographs so you can see some of the many sites that are mentioned in the book. Immediately I thought of my friend and colleague, Brian Morley. I had the privilege of leading Brian through the land of Israel as he took thousands of photographs with a professional expertise second to none. He is responsible for the striking cover as well as for the many well-chosen images that enhance the book.

Abundant gratitude goes to my wife Helen, my pastoral assistant Herald Gandi, and my friend Megan Smith for their valuable proofreading of a sometimes very rough manuscript. My final thanks goes to my editor and publisher, Todd Scacewater, who was there when I needed him during a tough time in my career.

1

THE BEGINNING OF THE VIA DOLOROSA

T he Gospels are crystal clear about the location of the beginning and the end of the last walk of Jesus to face his death. That trail of tears began in a building in Jerusalem, probably an annex of the original Herodian structure, where the Roman prefect Pontius Pilate condemned Jesus to die a horrific death reserved for murderous bandits and those who dared to revolt against Rome. These facts are familiar to most people and precious to every believing Christian because of their redemptive nature. But tradition has located the beginning of these events in different Herodian buildings. Actually, the final location of those events, *Golgotha*, is also debated, but that subject will come up later in this book. A tradition (you will read that word quite often in these pages) that dates only from the Middle Ages locates Pilate's Judgement Hall in the heart of the Muslim Quarter of the Old City of Jerusalem north of the area that Jews and Christians call the Temple Mount. This was the site of the Antonia Fortress that features later as the place where Paul was rescued from a near lynching and from where he was whisked away by night to escape an assassination plot (Acts 21). Tradition has it that in the barracks of the Antonia Fortress, Jesus was scourged and mocked and forced to carry at least the beam of a cross to Golgotha.

Figure 1: The Phasael Tower, built by Herod the Great, was part of the residence of the Roman Procurator. The site was also the Praetorium where Pilate judged Jesus (John 18:28–19:16), and where the soldiers mocked and beat him (Matt 27:27–31).

Although scholars today place Pilate's condemnation of Jesus near what is today's Jaffa Gate, my purpose is not to enter into that debate at this point. What I want you to imagine is a path from east to west, less than a mile in length, that winds through the Muslim Quarter and ends in the Christian Quarter at the Church of the Holy Sepulcher. That path has been memorialized as the *Via Dolorosa*, Latin for "way of sorrows." At over a dozen spots of that *way* are little shrines important to Roman Catholics as the Stations of the Cross. These *stations* are based on events in the Gospels such as Simon of Cyrene's bearing the cross (Mark 15:21), but also on some imaginary legends such as Veronica's Veil, which she supposedly placed on the Lord's face and was miraculously imprinted with an image of his face! Roman Catholic pilgrims, especially on Good Friday, reverently trace these stations of the cross as an act of piety and devotion.

I want to argue, however, that the real beginning of our Lord's physical sufferings on that fateful day was not the first station on the traditional *Via Dolorosa* in Jerusalem. The beginning of our Lord's "way of sorrows" actually took place maybe six months prior and a hundred and fifty miles to the north of Jerusalem, at a site known in the Gospels as Caesarea Philippi near the northern border of Israel today. There were two ancient "Caesareas" and you can visit them both when, not *if*, you visit the land of Israel. Caesarea Maritima, as its name expresses, is the Caesarea by the sea (the Mediterranean), between Haifa to the north and Tel Aviv to the south. It was built by Herod the Great and is one of the major stops on every visit to Israel. (At the time I am writing this, I and my wife are leading a group there tomorrow!) Caesarea Philippi, on the other hand, was built by Philip, Herod the Great's son, and named that to distinguish it from the larger Caesarea on the coast built by his father. This latter town was known to the Greeks as *Paneas*, named that to recall the spring gushing from a cave in honor of Pan, the god of the springs and nymphs. Arabs call the site *Banyas* because they pronounce the "p" sound as a "b."

Figure 2: Jesus withdrew to Caesarea Philippi, a Gentile city, for intimate time with his disciples. Here he began to reveal that he must suffer, making this in essence the beginning of the Via Delorosa.

The Synoptic Gospels each place the great confession of Jesus as Messiah (*Christos*) at this important site, "far away from the maddening crowd" in Jesus' day.

Now for some important context about the Great Galilean ministry of Jesus that lasted about a year and a half. Jesus made three missionary and preaching tours in Galilee, lasting about a year in total. In these tours his ministry of preaching and healing was very public in the towns of Galilee, mainly around the *Yam Kinneret* or Sea of Galilee. During one of those tours was the first great turning point in the Galilee ministry, when Jesus was accused of performing his miracles through the power of Satan (Matt 12:24–26). After this serious charge, the ministry of Jesus became focused more on parables that actually hid the truth from outsiders but were clear to those who understood the mystery of the kingdom (Matt 13). This public preaching and healing ministry was then followed by four withdrawals, in each of which Jesus instructed almost exclusively only the twelve disciples.

The withdrawal to Caesarea Philippi—the fullest account of which is given in Matthew 16—is the last of these withdrawals, each of which was to a predominantly Gentile area. As Jesus and the disciples withdrew to this area for more intimate and personal instruction, Jesus asked them an important question: "Who do people say that I am?" They answered that some were opting for Elijah and some for one of the prophets. Jesus' second question was more direct: "Who do *you* say that I am?" Peter responded that Jesus was the Messiah, the Son of the living God. Jesus then pronounces Peter as blessed and offers a promise that "upon this rock I will build my church and the gates of Hades will not prevail against it." Most Protestant evangelicals, sensitive to Rome's teaching that Peter was the first pope, steer away from any idea that Peter could be the rock, although Peter's name in Greek actually means "stone" or "rock." There was a real sense in which Peter served a foundational role in the early history of the church. His prominent role in Acts 1–12 is quite evident to all readers. Where we differ with Rome is that Peter eventually faded from any prominent role after Acts 12, and also never fulfilled any role as a forgiver of sins or one who accepted the reverence of other followers of Jesus the Messiah. As a matter of fact, he even discouraged Cornelius from bowing to him, saying that he was just a man (Acts 10:26). If we dare to speak of Peter's primacy, it was actually only a chronological and not a hierarchical primacy. Careful readers of the Book of Acts recognize that, at least from Acts 12 onward, it was James who was the human head of the early Christian movement, not Peter.

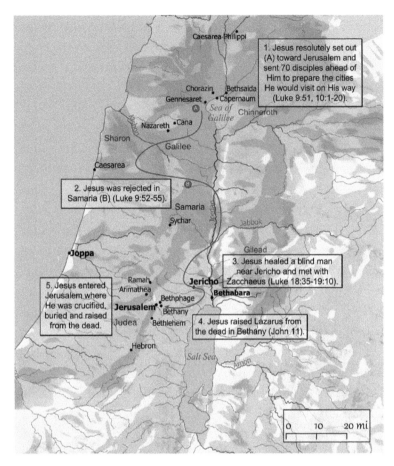

Figure 3: The Via Dolorosa *beginning at Caesarea Philippi and ending in Jerusalem. Created by Joe Anderson, used by permission.*

But how did the *Via Dolorosa* start here at Caesarea Philippi? Immediately after his response to Peter, the text of Matthew gives us that answer: "From that time on Jesus began to explain to his disciples that he must go to Jerusalem and suffer many things at the hands of the elders, the chief priests and the teachers of the law, and that he must be killed and on the third day be raised to life" (Matt 16:21). Matthew is very specific that "from that time on" Jesus taught about his coming suffering which came to its full fruition in the events of the Passion Week, especially on Thursday night and Friday. This event at Caesarea Philippi was the second main *turning point* in Jesus' Galilean ministry because of this new theme in his teaching, namely that he would soon suffer and die as the rejected Messiah. The Gospels record at least two more explicit predictions of his *passion* in the coming months as he steadfastly set his face toward Jerusalem and the passion that awaited him (Luke 9:51). These predictions found their fulfillment as Jesus trod the path that is called today the *Via Dolorosa*. And that *Via* actually began here, a hundred and fifty miles away from Jerusalem in Caesarea Philippi.

I have always been struck by how the disciples just did not *get it* about the coming suffering of Jesus. Even to the end and after his resurrection, they just did not recognize that Jesus was headed toward rejection and death as the suffering servant of Isaiah. But why should I be shocked when here at the beginning of the *Via Dolorosa* Peter actually rebuked Jesus for stating such an outrageous idea? Peter took him aside and began to rebuke him. "Never, Lord!" he said. "This shall never happen to you! Jesus turned and said to Peter, 'Get behind me, Satan! You are a stumbling block to me; you do not have in mind the concerns of God, but merely human concerns.' Then Jesus said to his disciples, 'Whoever wants to be my disciple must deny themselves and take up their cross and follow me'" (Matt 16:22–24).

Long ago I heard a preacher say that if Peter was the spiritual head of the church and the first pope, then the church was founded on Satan! Actually Jesus was expressing that the meaning of Satan, "adversary," was the role that Peter was playing, that of an adversary to the Divine plan that the Lord's Messiah was to suffer and die a violent death for our sins. It was not a beautiful piece of jewelry hanging around our neck that Jesus told us to bear. It was a cross that meant death, even as it was his cross that lay at the end of the original *Via Dolorosa*. And that way of sorrows actually began months before, in Caesarea Philippi.*

———————▼———————

*For further study of the geographical aspects of Jesus' life, see Donald L. Brake and Todd Bolen, *Jesus, A Visual History: The Dramatic Story of the Messiah in the Holy Land* (Zondervan, 2014).

Suggested Prayer: "Lord Jesus, the path that you travelled on your personal "Way of Sorrows" was a road you walked for me. Luke tells me that you set your face like a flint toward Jerusalem, although knowing what lay ahead. Thank you, dear Savior, for not backing down from that task and not shirking what your Father had ordained for you to do. May I take up my cross daily and follow you down that same path."

Figure 4: Model of Jerusalem as it was in Jesus' day, before it was destroyed in AD 70. Israel Museum.

2

PALM MONDAY?

For nearly two thousand years, Christians of all stripes and flavors have observed the events of that last week of Jesus in Jerusalem with a special interest and focus. As I mentioned earlier, some Christians call it *Holy Week* and some *Passion Week*, while others simply prefer the "Last Week." Whatever be the title (the Gospels use none of those expressions), the fateful period marks its beginning with what is often called the *Triumphal Entry* of Jesus into Jerusalem on what has come to be called *Palm Sunday*. I again remind the reader that none of these expressions are used by the Biblical authors, but they are still useful for referring to the week.

In this chapter we will begin our examination of some of the events in Passion Week that deserve a closer look. The first item deserving closer inspection is the idea that Jesus made his formal entry into Jerusalem, mentioned in each of the Gospels, on a Sunday. Because of the use of branches laid before Jesus as he entered on a donkey (only John mentions that they were palm branches, 12:13), the expression "Palm Sunday" arose. But was the entrance really on a Sunday? Even at the risk of making some readers anxious, I suggest that the entry most probably took place on a Monday. I know that changing our time-worn terminology to "Palm Monday" will be hard, but I will simply use "Triumphal Entry" for the important event. Before we look at the issue, I want to write that knowing the exact day is not going to cause any cherished beliefs to be threatened. This is not an issue to break fellowship over! But recognizing the day as Monday may help a few things to fall in line.

As we progress through the week, you will notice that traditional chronologies are forced to make Wednesday a day of silence regarding our Lord's activities. In this approach, after delivering his Olivet Discourse on Tuesday afternoon, Jesus "goes dark" until the Last Passover/Supper with his disciples on Thursday evening. Wednesday has no events since most everyone accepts that the Gospels mention of an anointing at Simon's house is a flashback to the past Saturday evening in Bethany. But such a return to Bethany, which is east of the Mount of Olives, would conflict with the statements that Jesus stayed his last few nights on the Mount of Olives, not in Bethany (Luke 21:37; 22:39). That is how Judas knew where to take the officers to arrest Jesus, because he knew that he had been staying there (Gethsemane)—but we are getting ahead of ourselves!

Some point to the fact that Jesus' arrival in the Jerusalem area six days before Passover (John 12:1) would point to a Saturday arrival in Bethany and a Sunday entrance into Jerusalem. But those six days only mention his arrival in Bethany. Evidently Jesus spent the next day (Sunday) in Bethany greeting a great crowd who came there to see him and to see Lazarus, whom Jesus had earlier raised from the dead (John 12:9–11). Then the next day (Monday) he entered Jerusalem (John 12:12). Not only does this suggested chronology do away with the need to create a silent day on Wednesday, but it also works better with the often-overlooked fulfillment of the typology of the ancient Passover lamb.

Figure 5: A tradition identifies the Golden Gate with Ezekiel 43:4 and the entry to the Temple through which the Messiah will come. Crusaders unblocked it every year to celebrate Christ's Triumphal Entry. Built in the 6ᵗʰ or 7ᵗʰ century, it stands on the ruins of a much older gate.

If the entry into Jerusalem was on Monday, the day of the entry would be Nisan 10 when the lamb was selected for the coming Passover on Nisan 14. If you count back from the Friday when the lamb was killed, it would be selected and set aside on Monday, Nisan 10 (Exod 12:3). Hence, the Triumphal Entry was the day that the Messiah presented himself as Israel's Paschal Lamb. He was set aside to be the Passover Lamb on Nisan 10 (Monday), and sacrificed as the Passover Lamb on Nisan 14 (Friday).

What else can be said about the Triumphal Entry that might shed some light on the details of its significance? Matthew 21:5 reminds the reader that the event took place "to fulfill what was spoken by the prophet saying…," and then he cites Zechariah 9:9: "Rejoice greatly, O daughter of Zion! Shout aloud, O daughter of

Jerusalem! Behold, your king is coming to you; righteous and having salvation is he, humble and mounted on a donkey, on a colt, the foal of a donkey." The Gospel of John also mentions the words from the prophet but neither writer actually gives the name of the prophet that they are quoting. Because the prophet is not mentioned by name, many casual Bible readers do not realize that Zechariah 9 is being quoted. Even fewer have taken the time to examine the context of the Zechariah passage, especially the preceding verses of 9:1–8. I personally have never heard a preacher preach from Zechariah 9 on "Palm Sunday." Neglecting that context means that we miss an important comparison and also a vivid contrast.

I invite the reader to look at Zechariah 9:1–8 and see if you can conclude who is being prophesied about in those earlier verses. If you know anything about one of the most important persons in history, you will soon recognize that it is a remarkable prophecy about another king, a Gentile Macedonian named Alexander the Great. What then develops before you is a rather detailed description in advance of the inexorable march of that world conqueror through the Middle East. The fascinating thing is that what we read meshes exactly with what the historians tell us about the king's brutal itinerary. First he ravished Syria (9:1–2a), then the area that we know today as Lebanon (9:2b–4). Even the fascinating account of how he built an artificial breakwater out to that Phoenician island fortress of Tyre is described as striking down her power in the sea. His march down the coast to the old Philistine cities is graphically foretold (9:5–7), even the death of the king of Gaza, the only enemy king that Alexander executed. Then in 9:8, contrary to the preceding verses, is a description of how God will spare his house in Jerusalem (9:8). The Greek historians tell us that Alexander did not destroy Jerusalem. A legend related by Josephus and the Talmud informs us that the high priest Jaddua met Alexander and impressed him so much that the priest was allowed to show him from the books of Daniel and Zechariah that his successful career was actually prophesied by the Jewish God! You can reject that story if you wish, but we do know from those same Greek sources that Alexander relieved the Jews of the harsh taxes he imposed on other conquered peoples and did not force them to serve in his forces. Now why haven't you heard these amazing things that form the background of the Triumphal Entry on Palm Sunday, uh, Monday?

One last intertextual connection should be mentioned. The crowds also shouted "Hosanna ... blessed is he who comes in the name of the Lord" (Matt 21:9). It is easily overlooked that this expression is also a quotation from the Old Testament, specifically from Psalm 118:25–26, a psalm that merits your own further study. It is often overlooked that this great statement in the psalm will be cited twice more explicitly by the Lord Jesus in the next two days (Matt 21:42; 23:39). Then it will be implicitly cited at the conclusion of the event that Christians call the Last Supper on Thursday night (Mark 14:26). More on that great psalm later. This mention of that text is just a preview of coming attractions!

We must end this chapter with a sad footnote. Mobs of Jesus' followers, both those pilgrims from Galilee and some Jerusalemites (and we will argue that there were more of them in Jerusalem than most people often recognize), hailed him as their Messiah. But there were others who strongly demurred. To be accepted as the Messiah of the nation of Israel demanded that Israel's national leaders also hail him in this manner. Sadly, the leaders refused to do so. Two Gospel writers record the jealousy and perplexity of those leaders at this moment (Luke 19:39; John 12:19). These religious leaders, especially the Sadducees, had previously already made up their minds about him (John 11:47–53, 57).

On the slope of the Mount of Olives, just off the path that Jesus descended that day, is a beautiful chapel named the Dominus Flevit, Latin for "the Lord wept." The chapel is architecturally designed to remind the visitor of a tear drop, even with the ancient tear bottles included in the outside corners of the building exterior. It commemorates the touching plea that Jesus issued to the Jewish people as he descended that slope. His words are found in Luke 19:41–42: "As he approached Jerusalem and saw the city, he wept over it and said, 'If you, even you, had only known on this day what would bring you peace—but now it is hidden from your eyes.'" Jesus knew very well what lay ahead of him, namely his rejection by the Jewish leadership and the eventual destruction of their beloved Jerusalem by the Romans, ironically the same people who would condemn and execute him in just a few days! And the thought of that caused him to weep!

It is my prayer that the Triumphal Entry will now be even richer to your heart and soul by closely considering these things, which are not hidden but are often simply overlooked.*

▼

*The NT scholar Harold W. Hoehner argued effectively for the above chronology of the Passion Week in *Chronological Aspects of the Life of Christ* (Zondervan, 1977), 90–139.

Suggested Prayer: "Lord Jesus, the multitudes welcomed you as the fulfillment of Zechariah's prophecy. As you received their praises, you paused and wept over Jerusalem because its leaders did not join in that welcome song. May my heart also weep over the unbelief of my friends and neighbors who still do not recognize who you are. Hasten the day when they join in the chorus of 'Blessed is he who comes in the name of the Lord.'"

3

How Did He Get Away With It?
The Cleansing of the Temple

The dramatic scene has been captured often by artists—a man with a whip in his hands amidst the shock and awe of the vendors as they watch their tables being over-turned, their animals loosed, and their money rolling away. It is the vivid scene of Jesus *cleansing the Temple*. What is going on here? And then comes the question that is not always asked: how did he get away with such destruction? It is time to review the major role that the Temple had in Jesus' day and how such a scene that so enraged Jesus came into being. Was this more than just an outburst of anger? Was there any religious significance to this act? Finally we will take a closer look at how he was able to get away with such a public display of destruction and mayhem.

The first Temple was constructed under the reign of Solomon, son of King David (1 Kings 6–9), and it was destroyed by the Babylonians in 586 BC. After their return from the resulting exile, Zerubbabel led the Jewish effort to rebuild the Temple, with the approval of their new masters, the Persians. Although it was not as glorious as Solomon's great structure, it provided the place for the renewed sacrifices under the leadership of a renewed priesthood from the Zadokite family (Ezra 8–10; Neh 12–13). The "Second Temple," as it came to be called, actually served for over four hundred years until it was greatly enlarged and beautified by that Builder of Builders, Herod the Great (approx. 30–20 BC). It continued to be worked on through the ministry of Jesus and was not actually completely finished until around AD 64. This magnificent structure then came crashing down in August, AD 70, never afterward to be reconstructed. Technically, therefore, the Herodian Temple was the third one, but scholars still call it the Second Temple because Zerubbabel's Temple was never destroyed by an enemy.

Now who ran the Temple? Knowing that answer will provide us with some great insight into why Jesus was so annoyed at what he witnessed going on there. The priests in the OT were descendants of Aaron through his descendant Zadok. That Zadokite line continued into the intertestamental period, but during the time of the Maccabees (2nd century BC), descendants of Aaron through a non-Zadok line took over not only the high priestly role but even usurped the kingly role which was reserved for the tribe of Judah (Gen 49:10). The Jewish sect of the Essenes rejected this illegitimate line of high priests and dropped out of Jerusalem society by heading for the area of Qumran on the Dead Sea. They even referred to themselves as the legitimate "Sons of Zadok." During Herod the Great's reign, he appointed high priests that were also not in the legitimate line and they continued to rule, with the family of Annas dominant in Jerusalem until the Temple's destruction. These descendants of Annas, including his son Caiaphas who oversaw Jesus' trial, were corrupt leaders put in power and kept there by the Romans themselves. One can even see their privileged and "kept by the Romans" position described by Caiaphas himself in John 11:47–53.

One of the ways in which this corrupt religious leadership funded its wealth was through the exorbitant income they received through their Temple "business." A huge part of that business was directly related to Jesus' act of cleansing—the sale of animals and the exchange of currency. People needed to buy sacrificial animals, especially the lambs at Passover. They also needed to exchange the currency that they used in their home countries to pay the annual Temple tax in the shekel currency of Jerusalem. These activities were actually necessary actions, but the Sadducees and priestly leaders maneuvered these things to their own advantage. They even allowed the vendors into the Temple area, specifically the huge Court of the Gentiles (part of the larger *hieron*) which surrounded the Temple proper (the *naos*).

Of course, their allowing the vendors into the Temple area came with a price, specifically a cut of the money that the vendors received from their price-gouging of the common people. Huge over-charging thus took place for an animal and a huge commission fee was charged for the money changing. And guess who profited from that? Later rabbis in the Talmud even mocked this practice by referring to the business derisively as the "Bazaar of the Sons of Annas." Sincere worshippers were taken advantage of and simply ripped off in the process. These Jewish worshippers faced this corruption in the very place where they should have been able to openly and freely experience one of the highlights of their lives—a visit to the holiest place on earth, the Temple of Yahweh. So what do they see there? They hear a cacophony of salesmen hawking their wares as in the marketplace of any Middle Eastern bazaar you can visit today, probably even worse. And what of the Gentiles who might visit, since they were allowed into this very Court of the Gentiles? Instead of beholding the beauty of the Jewish House of the One True God, they encountered this noise and corruption.

Some people have the impression that Jesus cleansed the Temple immediately after the Triumphal Entry on Monday, but both Matthew and Mark say that it was the next day, or Tuesday

Figure 6: In Jesus' day, the expanse of the Court of the Gentiles around the Temple would have been filled with people, merchants, and money changers. The location of the stairs, the top of which can be seen on the right, dates from antiquity.

morning (Matt 21:8–12; Mark 11:12–15). Mark says that Jesus, after his entry into the city, simply looked around the Temple and then returned to Bethany (Mark 11:11). I like to think that he was observing the awful mess in the Temple courtyard and then was determining his plans for the next day. It is Mark, the shortest Gospel, that actually gives the most detailed description of the cleansing (Mark 11:15–18). As was the case in so many of the decisive acts of our Lord, there was an Old Testament background that lent urgency to and contributed the spiritual meaning to his actions. Jesus declared as he began to clear this mess that Yahweh had affirmed his house should be a house of prayer for *all* nations, a reference to that declaration in Isaiah 56:7. Do you see how powerful that statement was in light of the fact that this "bazaar" of vendors were doing their thing in the Court of the *Gentiles*? When Gentile visitors came to the Temple (and they did, John 12:20–21), instead of seeing the beauty of Israel's God, they were greeted by this sordid mess of thieving hawkers, marketing their wares. Jesus also accused the leaders, not just the vendors, that they had transformed the house of Yahweh into "a robber's den." Readers with their spiritual antennae up should recognize a clear allusion to Jeremiah's "temple sermon" in Jeremiah 7:11. Just as Jeremiah had condemned the spiritual idolatry in that First Temple, so Jesus confronted the monetary idolatry in this Second Temple.

But I still have not answered the question I posed as the title of this chapter: How did he get away with this? It is evident that the leaders hated his attack on this their illegitimate "business" (Mark 11:18; Luke 19:47). There existed at the time a strong force of "Temple Police" who managed any troublemakers in this *holy* site. Why were they not ordered to intervene and stop this Galilean rabble-rouser who was wrecking their profits? I think they did try to prevent him, but something prevented them from apprehending him. I am amazed at how often Christians fall back on Divine intervention in subjects like this. "Well, the Lord just prevented them by his power from stopping Jesus." I do not doubt that, but the text states clearly *how* that took place. Immediately after describing the cleansing, Luke adds: "But the chief priests, the teachers of the law and the leaders among the people were trying to kill him. *Yet they could not find any way to do it, because all the people hung on his words*" (Luke 19:47–48). And notice Matthew 21:46: "They looked for a way to arrest him, but they were afraid of the crowd because the people held that he was a prophet" (see also Mark 12:12 and Luke 20:19). They were not prevented by some invisible power emanating from Jesus; they were prevented by a horde of common people surrounding the Savior, who were hanging on his very words.

In my experience of hearing sermons and even hearing teachers of the life of Jesus, these verses are so often overlooked. I can imagine with some firm basis that wherever Jesus went through the court as he was teaching the next two days, that a cadre of young men was surrounding him, making sure that he was safe from those who would have liked to seize him. Remember that when we consider the fateful events on the following Thursday evening, when the Temple police did successfully seize Jesus while he was away from the adoring crowds in the darkness of Gethsemane. Remember this also when we address later one of the most serious charges leveled against his Jewish followers, namely that they were *fickle* by changing from hailing him as Messiah on Monday and then crying for his blood on Friday morning. They didn't change. That was a different crowd on Friday. This is one of the most often overlooked facts so clearly mentioned in the Gospels that I am shocked that so many forget or ignore it. "The large crowd listened to him with delight" (Mark 12:37), or as the KJV has it: "And the common people heard him gladly."

One last remark about Jesus and the Temple still remains, and it is about the interesting cursing of the fig tree. Mark 11:12–21 makes it clear that the cursing and the subsequent withering of the tree were two separate events, and it is fascinating that the two incidents actually surround the narration of the cleansing of the Temple. The two actions must be seen in connection with each other and in connection with the Temple judgement. The parable in Isaiah 5:1–7 is the background, namely that Israel as the fig tree should be showing fruit but they did not and thus they were judged. The most "showy" branch of Israel's tree was the Temple and it would be in that sacred space where fruit should be expected to be seen. Alas, no fruit was there, only rotten behavior, and behavior that was even encouraged by Israel's leaders. The fig tree and the Temple cleansing work together as an acted-out parable of judgment. One final comment on Jesus' lesson about prayer that strangely is appended to the withering of the fig tree. "Truly, I say to you, if you have faith and do not doubt, you will not only do what has been done to the fig tree, but even if you say to this mountain, 'Be taken up and thrown into the sea,' it will happen" (Matt 21:21; also Mark 11:22–23). For years I could not see the connection of this statement with the cursing of the fig tree, but then I realized its close connection with the Temple. Jewish people call the site of the Temple the *Har Habayit*, the Temple Mount, Mount Moriah of the Old Testament (2 Chron 3:1). If Jesus' followers had the appropriate faith, then they would see the awful judgement of the Temple being symbolically cast into the sea. In other words, the destruction of this mighty edifice, so polluted by the religious leadership, would be the fulfillment of the prophetic word to Zechariah: "What are you, mighty mountain? Before Zerubbabel you will become level ground" (4:7).

Jesus' spiritual pronouncement of judgement of the Temple became a foreshadowing of its eventual physical judgment because it had become nothing more than "a den of robbers." He got away with it because there was a host of common people who believed in him—and protected him! This continued until his enemies found him later one night almost completely alone.*

------▼------

*For additional insights into the last days of Jesus, see Craig Evans, *Jesus and the Remains of His Day: Studies in Jesus and the Evidence of Material Culture* (Hendrickson, 2015).

Suggested prayer: "Lord Jesus, you were justly enraged by this crass lack of reverence in your house. Help me to realize that you, the loving Lord Jesus, were filled with righteous anger by these awful abuses. Help me to hate sin in all its forms. Show me how to hate sin with a perfect hatred, while still loving the sinner with the perfect love that you have. I cannot do this without your help."

4

A PHARISEE IS NOT SAD-YOU-SEE

A third-century rabbi, reflecting on the past history of his people, plaintively remarked, "Israel went into exile only after it became divided into twenty-four sects" (Jerusalem Talmud, *Sanhedrin* 29c). Although we cannot be sure of the exact number, there can be no doubt that at the time of the destruction of the Temple (AD 70) Judaism was divided into many sects. Modern historians also uphold his view that the downfall of the Jewish state was the direct consequence of its internal disunity. It is the purpose of this chapter to become more familiar with these groups because Jesus encountered all of them in one way or another. This becomes very intense on Wednesday morning, the events of which are recorded in Matthew 22 and 23.

In the first century Jewish world in Jerusalem there were groups of Sadducees, Essenes, Zealots, and Herodians, plus the vast majority of common people who belonged to no religious sect at all. The most famous group he encountered, however, was the **Pharisees.** This group was the most significant sect of Jesus' day, and their specific role during the Passion Week is fascinating to examine, and there may be some surprises ahead of us when we do so. While their membership only totaled a few thousand,

Figure 7: When Jesus called hostile Pharisees "whitewashed tombs"—attractive on the outside but unclean—people could think of the prominent graves in the Kidron Valley. The so-called "Tomb of Absalom" was built in the early first century.

their influence was felt far beyond their numbers. Often associated with the scribes, who were professional scholars in the Jewish law, the Pharisees received the most stinging rebukes Jesus ever issued. At least seven times in Matthew 23, Jesus pronounced the following condemnation: "Woe unto you, scribes and Pharisees, hypocrites!" He condemned their rapaciousness, their selfishness, their inward spiritual emptiness, and their emphasis on scruples while neglecting the *big* matters of justice, mercy, and faith. These excoriating denunciations have resulted in the word *Pharisee* entering the English language as a synonym for *hypocrite*.

Did Jesus unjustly criticize the Pharisees for sins of which they were not guilty? Let us first see *what the Pharisees said about themselves.* There are descriptions of the Pharisees in Josephus and in the Babylonian and Jerusalem Talmuds. Flavius Josephus, himself a Pharisee, described the group as (1) being meticulous about observing the law, both in its written and oral forms; (2) affirming the immortality of the soul and the resurrection of the body; and (3) having greater influence on the common people than the other sects (*Antiquities of the Jews* 18.1). It is the Pharisaic emphasis on the oral law, called the "tradition" in the Gospels, with which Jesus had the greatest conflict. See, for example, Matthew 15:1–9.

Talmudic sources state that there were different kinds of Pharisees—seven to be exact (Talmud, *Berachot* 14b). What is surprising is that six of the seven Pharisees were *bad*, and this was according to their own estimation. (The compilers of the Talmud were most directly the descendants of the Pharisees.) This self-description sounds as harsh as some of Jesus' judgments on this group! Therefore, when Jesus castigated some of the Pharisees for hypocrisy and false piety, he was only pointing out what the Pharisees recognized about many of their own members. Doubtless there were *good* Pharisees, who lived up to their ideals. The seventh group in the Talmud, the "God-loving" Pharisees, may have been in a minority, but they do occasionally appear in the New Testament. In Luke 13:31 we read, "At that very hour some Pharisees came and said to him, 'Get away from here, for Herod wants to kill you.'" This passage shows that even among the Pharisees there were those who admired and respected Jesus. Furthermore, Nicodemus and Joseph of Arimathea, who became believers in the Lord Jesus, were probably Pharisees, as well as Saul, known later as Paul (John 3:1; 7:50; 19:38–39; Acts 22:3; Phil 3:5). Therefore, Jesus' condemnation of the Pharisees was not universal. The Pharisees were not all bad, even though many were. Jesus' strong statements at times were consistent with the Pharisees' recognition that they often fell far short of their own ideals.

In the generation prior to Jesus, there lived two great Pharisees, each of whom led a school of thought in Jerusalem: Hillel and Shammai. Shammai followed a more rigid and harsh interpretation of the law, while Hillel expounded a more flexible interpretation'. This conflict between the strict and freer Pharisaic interpretations of the law is also reflected in their question to Jesus regarding divorce, "And Pharisees came up to him and tested him by asking, 'Is it lawful to divorce one's wife for any cause?'" (Matt 19:3). The text that the Pharisee students were appealing to was Deuteronomy 24:1–4. Shammai taught that the "indecency" mentioned in Deuteronomy 24:1 that could justify putting away one's wife could only be sexual indecency. Hillel, on the other hand, had a much broader interpretation of the "indecency" that could justify divorce. In addition to sexual unfaithfulness, these acts could include all kinds of real and imagined offenses, including even an improperly cooked meal!

Please note that in condemning the Pharisees Jesus was not condemning the entire group, but only the bad ones, even though they may have constituted a majority of the membership. Furthermore, Jesus' condemnation of some of the Pharisaic practices may sometimes reflect the stringent, hyper-strict scruples of some schools within the Pharisees—Shammai's teachings for example. The emphasis that I am stressing may be new to some readers and could be to my Christian readers the most controversial point I have made. I am not trying to whitewash the Pharisees, since Jesus' words about them were true and well directed. I am just trying to understand those pointed words in the context of *all* that is said about the Pharisees in the Gospels and in the contemporary Judaism of Jesus' day.

This background on the Pharisees informs a very important event that took place on Wednesday morning of Passion Week. Jesus was confronted in the Temple area by a contingent of different groups, each seeking to ask him a question. The account is found in Matthew 22:15–46. The groups who approached Jesus were the Herodians, the Sadducees and the Pharisees, three of the various sects and parties among the first-century Jewry. The questions they asked were meant to "entangle him in his talk" (v. 15). These were not sincere inquiries after the truth, but were questions designed to either embarrass Jesus or cause him to contradict himself. Let us see how Jesus responded to them.

The **Herodians** were a Jewish political party who supported the Herod dynasty which had been ruling the Jewish people as "puppet kings" since 37 BC. It was appropriate, therefore, that their question was of a political nature: "Tell us, then, what you think. Is it lawful to pay taxes to Caesar, or not?" (v. 17). The question they raised was a burning issue for every Jew during that time, because part of their responsibility to the Roman rulers was the payment of a head tax. There was a great amount of discussion among Jews over this tax, for they recognized only Yahweh as their legitimate King.

Their motive for asking Jesus was to "entangle him in his talk." They were attempting to put Jesus on the horns of a dilemma. If he answered, "Yes, it is lawful to pay the tax," then he would lose favor with the common people who despised Herod and the Romans. If he answered, "No, it is not lawful to pay the tax," then they would report him to the Roman authorities as an inciter of treason. Jesus asked for a "denarius," the coin used to pay the tax, and pointed out the embossed image of Tiberius Caesar, the Roman Emperor who reigned from AD 14 to 37. Then came his classic answer, "Therefore render to Caesar the things that are Caesar's, and to God the things that are God's" (v. 21). In this simple yet profound statement, Jesus enunciated a principle which is confirmed elsewhere in the New Testament—the distinction between our political and spiritual responsibilities (Rom 12:1–7; 1 Pet 2:13–17). In other words, he says, "Your money has Caesar's image on it, therefore, it belongs to Caesar. Your soul, however, has God's image on it; therefore, it belongs to God." Instead of entangling Jesus in his words, the Herodians "marveled, and they left him and went away."

"The same day **Sadducees** came to him, who say that there is no resurrection..." (v. 23). The membership of the Sadducees was largely from the priesthood and upper classes (cf. Acts 4:1; 5:17). Unlike the Pharisees, who put great emphasis on oral tradition, the Sadducees "hold that only those regulations should be considered valid which were written down in the Torah" (Josephus, *Antiquities* 14.297). They put great emphasis on the first five books of Moses, which, they said, did not teach the resurrection of the body and immortality of the soul (Matt 23:2; Acts 4:2; 23:8). On the other hand, because the Pharisees *did* believe in the resurrection, they were not Sad-You-See!

The question these leaders addressed to Jesus intended to show the foolishness of the resurrection. They cited the Levirate law of Deuteronomy 25:5–10, which states that a deceased man's brother should marry the surviving widow, and presented a hypothetical situation of a woman who had been widowed seven times, her husbands all being brothers. Such a disaster might prompt us today to check out the wife's cooking! However, the

Sadducees' purpose was to show that this would create quite a problem in the resurrection, for "in the resurrection, therefore, of the seven, whose wife will she be? For they all had her" (Matt 22:28).

There is no evidence that such an event ever took place, but the idea was probably taken from the Book of *Tobit*, a fanciful story of morality and piety that was then circulating among the Jewish people. In it a lady had been married a number of times without the marriage ever being consummated due to a demon killing her husbands! Whatever was the original source for this hypothetical "case," Jesus dealt with their question in a forthright manner. His response in Matthew 22:29–32 analyzed the error of the Sadducees as twofold. Their first error was that they misunderstood the nature of resurrection life, thinking that physical relationships in the world to come will be expressed in the same way as the relationships that we sustain on earth. Their second error was that they were ignorant that the Lord himself in Exodus 3:6 had proclaimed to Moses that he sustained a continuous, living relationship to the patriarchs who had long been dead. Thus, in the very Torah they recognized, the truth of immortality and resurrection was implicitly recognized. Matthew's concise and concluding statement simply needs no further comment. "And when the multitude heard this, they were astonished at his doctrine" (Matt 22:33).

The **Pharisees** must have been delighted when Jesus silenced their rivals, the Sadducees. The Pharisees composed the largest and most popular sect of Judaism. As was mentioned before, they firmly held to the "oral law," a large body of tradition that had been handed down for generations. Jesus referred to this body of oral law as "the tradition of the elders" (Matt 15:1–3; Mark 7:1–13). It involved many regulations regarding every area of religious practice and ritual purity. Since the Pharisees were the only Jewish

sect to survive the destruction of the Temple in AD 70, they for-
mulated the later rabbinic regulations of the Talmud, and today's
Orthodox Jews are their modern descendants.

"And one of them, a lawyer, asked him a question to test him.
'Teacher, which is the great commandment in the Law?'" (Matt
22:35–36). The Pharisees were constantly occupied with the law
(i.e., the "Torah"). They counted, classified, weighed and meas-
ured all the separate commandments of the moral, ceremonial,
and civil law. Through their computations, they had concluded
that there were 613 commandments, consisting of 248 positive
precepts (corresponding to the members of the body) and 365
negative precepts (answering to the days in a year)! Some of the
commandments were considered "heavy" and some were considered "light," and they debated which of these commandments
was the most important. In his infinite wisdom, the Lord Jesus
answered their query. "And he said to him, 'You shall love the
Lord your God with all your heart and with all your soul and with
all your mind. This is the great and first commandment. And a
second is like it: You shall love your neighbor as yourself. On
these two commandments depend all the Law and the Prophets"
(Matt 22:37–40).

Jesus quoted from one of the most familiar passages to the ob-
servant Jew, Deuteronomy 6:5, part of the *Shema,* the most basic
confessional prayer in all of Judaism, "Hear (*Shema*), O Israel, the
Lord our God, the Lord, is one. You shall love the LORD your God
with all your heart and with all your soul and with all your might"
(Deut 6:4–5). This verse expresses the vertical responsibility of
man to God. He then quoted from Leviticus 19:18, a verse which
expresses the horizontal relationship of man to man. In citing
these two commandments, Jesus was not exalting some commandments above others; he was summarizing the whole Torah as consisting of (1) love to God the Creator, and (2) love to

mankind, the Creation of God. We often speak of the "two tables of the law" as comprising the Ten Commandments—the first five expressing our responsibility to God and the last five our responsibility to others. Jesus refused to be caught up in the never-ending wrangling of the Pharisees about which commandment was "heaviest," etc. As a Jew faithful to the Hebrew Scriptures, he was simply echoing what the prophet had already stated, "He has told you, O man, what is good; and what does the LORD require of you but to do justice, and to love kindness, and to walk humbly with your God?" (Micah 6:8).

Having been on the receiving end of their questions, Jesus now turned the tables and confronted the Pharisees gathered around him with the most important question that a Jew can ever be asked. "Now while the Pharisees were gathered together, Jesus asked them a question, saying, 'What do you think about the Christ (i.e., the Messiah)? Whose son is he?' They said to him, 'The son of David.' He said to them, 'How is it then that David, in the Spirit, calls him Lord, saying, "The Lord said to my Lord, 'Sit at my right hand, until I put your enemies under your feet'"? If then David calls him Lord, how is he his son?'" (Matt 22:42–45).

The Pharisees had long ago concluded that the Messiah would be a descendant of David (2 Sam 7:12–16; Micah 5:2; Ps 132:11). The problem was that it just did not go far enough. Jesus did not deny that the Messiah would be David's son (Matt 1:1; 21:9; Luke 1:32). In citing the messianic prophecy in Psalm 110:1, he desired to show them that David also considered the Messiah as his "Lord." Thus, the One who was to be a human descendant of David was to be his divine Lord as well! The apparent contradiction in such a statement can only be comprehended if the Messiah was a God-Man—just what the Scriptures had predicted (Isa 9:6). Jesus of Nazareth, and only he, fulfilled such a marvelous description.

"And no one was able to answer him a word, nor from that day did anyone dare to ask him any more questions" (Matt 22:46). Such infinite wisdom must have had a spiritual effect on them as well. We read in later passages that such people as Nicodemus and Joseph of Arimathea were so affected by these and other claims of Jesus that they became his disciples, although secretly at first (John 3:1ff.; 7:45–52; 19:38–42; Luke 23:50–53). The early church in Jerusalem later included many members from the Pharisees (Acts 15:5), and the great Apostle Paul had himself been a Pharisee (Phil 3:5).

My final observation will be the most controversial suggestion thus far. At this point in the Synoptic Gospels, the Pharisees drop out of the account until after the burial (Matt 27:62). From Jesus' arrest through his condemnation and handing over to Pilate, the Sadducees and the high priestly rulers (also Sadducees) take center stage as those who engineer his condemnation. It is my contention that the Pharisees did not participate in the actual condemnation and crucifixion of Jesus. Please know that I am not attempting to whitewash the Pharisees, because Jesus condemned the hypocrisy of many of them as well as their stress on the oral law over the written law. I just ask that my readers consider the silence of the Synoptic Gospels regarding their role in Jesus' actual crucifixion. I am guessing that you were not expecting that final comment!*

*For further information on the ancient Jewish sects, see Anthony J. Saldarini, *Pharisees, Scribes and Sadducees* (Eerdmans, 2001.)

Suggested Prayer: "Lord Jesus, what boldness you showed in condemning the hypocrisy of the most religious people that you faced. While I also abominate this hypocrisy, may your words pierce into my own heart and reveal any hypocrisy lurking there. May I not be satisfied with cleaning the outside of my cup but confess and forsake the wickedness that lurks within my own heart."

5

TROUBLE IN THE TEMPLE

I t is now Wednesday afternoon and soon the Messiah will
"go dark." The morning controversies were his last public
ministry and the passage before us now records his last final
public appeal. As with so many important chapters in God's
Word, Matthew 24 actually begins at the end of the previous
chapter. The 23rd chapter is undoubtedly the hardest-hitting
message Jesus ever delivered during his earthly ministry. Eight
times in this chapter, Jesus, in the role of an Old Testament
prophet, pronounced judgment on some of the religious leaders
of his day by declaring, "Woe unto you, scribes and Pharisees,
hypocrites!" (Matt 23:13, 14, 15, 16, 23, 25, 27, 29). He condemned
their selfishness, rapaciousness, misguided zeal, legalism, lack of
inner spirituality, and persecution of God's prophets. The Jewish
leadership was simply following in the footsteps of their Old Testament forebears, who had treated God's earlier messengers as
they were now treating Jesus. "Therefore I send you prophets and
wise men and scribes, some of whom you will kill and crucify, and
some you will flog in your synagogues and persecute from town
to town, so that on you may come all the righteous blood shed on
earth, from the blood of innocent Abel to the blood of Zechariah

the son of Barachiah, whom you murdered between the sanctuary and the altar. Truly, I say to you, all these things will come upon this generation" (Matt 23:34–36).

His Plea

Although no stronger words ever came from the Savior, he concluded this blistering diatribe with one of the most tender, heartrending pleas recorded in all of Scripture: "O Jerusalem, Jerusalem, the city that kills the prophets and stones those who are sent to it! How often would I have gathered your children together as a hen gathers her brood under her wings, and you would not!" (Matt 23:37). Scripture offers no greater example of the uniting of divine holiness and divine love than this statement. After delivering a severe denunciation of sin, Jesus revealed a heart bursting with compassion for sinners. Israel's "chicks" refused the prophets' messages and thus refused to come under the protective wings of the mother hen! Now, in rejecting *the* Prophet, they were simply following their forebears. Another truth, although hypothetical, is clearly implied: if Israel had responded to Jesus' many invitations to come to salvation, he would have restored them to the land from which they had been dispersed for hundreds of years.

This was not the only time that Israel's Messiah wept over Jerusalem's unbelief. "And when he drew near and saw the city (on Monday), he wept over it, saying, 'Would that you, even you, had known on this day the things that make for peace! But now they are hidden from your eyes'" (Luke 19:41, 42). We mentioned earlier that on the western descent of the Mount of Olives there sits a lovely chapel called *Dominus Flevit* (Latin for "the Lord wept"). Commanding a magnificent view of the Temple Mount and the old city of Jerusalem, this chapel, built in the shape of a teardrop, recalls the broken heart of Jesus, who deeply loved this city and its people despite their unbelief. Adorning its altar is a beautiful mosaic portrayal of a hen gathering her chicks.

This plaintive statement revealing the heart of the Savior points out a valuable lesson about salvation. However people view the vexing problem of God's sovereign role in salvation as it relates to election and predestination, one fact is clear from Scripture: "Let us understand that the ruin of those who are lost is not because Christ was not willing to save them—nor yet because they wanted to be saved, but could not—but because they would not come to Christ. Let it be a settled principle that man's salvation is wholly of God and that man's ruin is wholly of himself" (J. C. Ryle, *Expository Thoughts on the Gospels*, vol. 1, (James Clarke & Co.: 1965), 311).

His Pronouncements

Jesus concluded his dramatic message to Jerusalem's religious leaders with two pronouncements. The first concerned the Temple, and the second concerned their attitude toward him. "See, your house is left to you desolate. For I tell you, you will not see me again, until you say, 'Blessed is he who comes in the name of the Lord'" (Matt 23:38–39).

Both of these pronouncements are rooted in Old Testament verses. In the first, Jesus pronounced judgment on the magnificent Temple where he had just given this message (see Matt 21:23; 24:1). It would be left *desolate*, devoid and empty, not only of people but of the Divine presence. Six hundred years earlier, the Prophet Jeremiah issued a similar statement about the first Jerusalem Temple: "But if you will not obey these words, I swear by myself, declares the LORD, that this house shall become a desolation" (Jer 22:5; see also Jer 12:7). As Jeremiah condemned the first Temple to destruction, Jesus condemned the second Temple in similar language. The fulfillment of this dreadful statement took place in AD 70 when the Temple Mount was desolated and destroyed by the Romans.

The second pronouncement (Matt 23:39) is the last public word Jesus gave to Israel. Jesus again cited the famous messianic text of Psalm 118:26: "Blessed is he who comes in the name of the LORD! We bless you from the house of the LORD." Another overlooked fact in Passion Week is the prominent role that Psalm 118 played in the message of Jesus. No less than four times during four fateful days and nights, this psalm came into view as part of the drama of redemption being enacted during those awesome days. We have not mentioned its culminating role at the end of a bluntly obvious parable (Matt 21:33–44, v. 42 quoting Ps 118:22–23). "And when the chief priests and elders heard his parables, they understood that he was speaking about them" (21:45). We will see Psalm 118 again portrayed implicitly on Thursday evening as part of the Passover Seder.

At this dramatic point, Jesus said to Israel's religious leaders in simple terms, "You have always rejected the messengers that God has sent to you. Now you have rejected me. I will no longer preach publicly to you. The next time you see me publicly will be when you have reversed your attitude about me. When you no longer say that I am the cursed one but that I am the blessed one, then I will reveal myself publicly to you again" (adapted from Matt 22:37–39). It is of interest to note that this was the last public ministry in which Jesus engaged during the week. The rest of the time before his crucifixion was spent in private ministry to his disciples.

This statement also anticipates the future national conversion of Israel spoken about so often in both the Old and New Testaments (see Hosea 5:14–15; Rom 11:26–27). In modern Hebrew, the terminology Jesus used, *Baruk Haba*, is literally translated "Blessed is he who comes," and is the everyday phrase in Israel for saying "Welcome!" In other words, at his first coming, Israel's leadership had posted a "Not Welcome" sign for their Messiah. When they change that sign to "Welcome," Jesus will return to them in power and glory (Rom 11:26–27).

His Prophecy

"Jesus left the temple and was going away. . ." (Matt 24:1a). This book is about the often-overlooked aspects of Passion Week. What is often overlooked is the connection between Matthew 23 and 24. Jesus' departure was not only physical; it was intended also to be symbolic. Jesus abandoned that magnificent structure, the scene of so many of his words and works, to its own desolation. At that point some of his disciples suddenly volunteered to become Jerusalem tour guides! " ... when his disciples came to point out to him the buildings of the Temple" (24:1b). Why would they want to show Jesus a building with which he was thoroughly familiar? Their action was no doubt motivated by the dramatic words they had just heard him utter about this Temple.

Jewish believer Alfred Edersheim, describes the scene so movingly:

> They had left the Sanctuary and the City, had crossed the Brook Kidron, and were slowly climbing the Mount of Olives. A sudden turn in the road, and the Sacred Building was once more in full view. Just then the western sun was pouring his golden beams on tops of marble cloisters and on the terraced courts and glittering on the golden spikes on the roof of the Holy Place. In the setting, even more than in the rising sun, must the vast proportions, the symmetry, and the sparkling sheen of this mass of snowy marble and gold have stood out gloriously. And across the black valley, and up the slopes of Olivet, lay the dark shadows of those gigantic walls

built of massive stones, some of them nearly twenty-four feet
long ... It was probably as they now gazed on all this gran-
deur and strength, that they broke the silence imposed on
them by gloomy thoughts of the near desolateness of that
House, which the Lord had predicted. One and another
pointed out to Him those massive stones and splendid buildings or spoke of the rich offerings with which the Temple
was adorned (Luke 21:5). It was but natural that the contrast
between this and the predicted desolation should have impressed them (*The Life and Times of Jesus the Messiah*, vol. 2
[Eerdmans, 1967], 431).

The Temple truly was impressive. Herod had constructed it of
white marble plated with gold, and it shone so brightly in the sun
that people could scarcely bear to look at it. Excavations around
the southwestern and southern walls of the Temple Mount have
revealed a small but graphic picture of the glory that marked this
structure. Surrounded by huge porticoes upheld by pillars of marble nearly 40 feet high, this Temple was the center of Judaism and
the pride of its people. The rabbis, who had no personal love for
the secular-minded Herod, even remarked, "He who has not seen
Herod's Temple has not seen a beautiful building" (Babylonian
Talmud, *Baba Batra*, 4a).

The disciples' actions reveal their thoughts about the incon-
gruity between what they saw and what they had just heard Jesus
say. Perhaps their minds were moving like this: "Did we hear you
correctly, Lord? Did you really mean that this marvelous building
will someday be empty, deserted, and desolate?" Jesus was une-
quivocal in his response to their offer of a guided tour of the Temple. "But he answered them, 'You see all these, do you not? Truly,
I say to you, there will not be left here one stone upon another
that will not be thrown down'" (Matt 24:2). No declaration could
have been expressed more clearly or fulfilled more literally.

Within 40 years of the time those words were uttered, they were graphically realized in an amazing manner.

In the spring of AD 70, the Roman legions, led by emperor Vespasian's son Titus, approached the Holy City in what would be the concluding chapter of a rebellion that had begun four years earlier. Camps were built, a siege wall constructed, and battering rams, catapults, and siege engines put in place. By August the walls were breached from the north, and the legionnaires poured into the Temple precincts in a wild frenzy. That beautiful Temple, which the disciples had so admired, exploded in a massive conflagration. When the flammable material had cooled, wrecking crews began their work of dismantling the stones that still remained. According to Josephus, the eyewitness historian, the pillars that supported the huge porticoes were 37 ½ feet high and so thick that three men linked together could not put their arms around them! Finely cut stones, some nearly 40 feet in length and weighing more than 100 tons, have been found beneath the remaining walls surrounding the Temple Mount.

The pillars were toppled, and the towers were wrecked. The paving stones were ripped up to get at the riches stored in the subterranean vaults. Tradition states that the gold that melted from the conflagration flowed between the flagstones and greedy soldiers systematically removed them for plunder. Thus, in a tragic but amazing manner, Jesus' words were literally fulfilled. Absolutely no remains of that magnificent structure are visible today. The stones of the Western Wall (called by Gentiles the "Wailing Wall"), the site of so many Jewish prayers today, were not part of the Temple itself but were lower courses of a retaining wall around the mount. According to Josephus, the city was dug up to such an extent that it was difficult to believe it had ever been inhabited.

The physical tragedy of the Temple's complete destruction is deepened by the spiritual tragedy that caused it. While rabbis later attributed its destruction to the sectarian conflict among the Jewish groups, Jesus gave another reason in Luke's synoptic parallel passage. "The days will come upon you, when your enemies will set up a barricade around you and surround you and hem you in on every side and tear you down to the ground, you and your children within you. And they will not leave one stone upon another in you, because you did not know the time of your visitation" (Luke 19:43–44). The last phrase could legitimately be paraphrased, "because you did not recognize the time of God's coming to you."

Israel's religious leaders rejected the Lord of glory and sowed the seeds of the eventual destruction of their Temple, their Sanhedrin, and their city. How tragic are the consequences of refusing to recognize God's Anointed One! It was this same Messiah who demonstrated his prophetic knowledge by predicting such a destruction that so dramatically was fulfilled.

Truly *the* Prophet was among us! See Deut 18:15–18 and Luke 7:16.*

▼

*For further information on the messianic role and deeds of Jesus, see the author's *The Messiah: Revealed, Rejected, Received* (AuthorHouse, 2004).

Suggested Prayer: "Lord Jesus, I stand in amazement that you foretold in detail the destruction of that amazing building, the Temple. Thank you for being a prophet as well as my priest and my king. I look forward to the end of all this. Hasten the day of your coming. May the fact of fulfilled prophecy encourage me to know that the future also is in your hands, and that I am part of that future blessedness."

Figure 8: When the Romans destroyed Jerusalem in AD 70, they pushed the giant ashlars down from the wall, where they lie today. This fulfilled Jesus' prophecy that "not one stone will be left on another that will not be thrown down" (Mark 13:2).

6

SINGING FOR YOUR SUPPER

O n Wednesday evening, following that dramatic discourse on the Mount of Olives, Jesus did not go back to
Bethany but spent the night in a special place called
Gethsemane. How do we know that? Let me put that answer off
until we examine the fateful events of the next night, Thursday,
which all are agreed centered on a fateful drama around Gethsemane.

The Gospels are clear that he sent disciples into the city on
Thursday morning to prepare for the Passover Seder, which he
desired to observe with them that evening. The disciples had to
do two things. First, they had to secure a lamb, have it killed in
the Temple, secure provisions for the Passover meal, and then ar-
range for the meal to be prepared. Second, they had to secure a
room large enough to accommodate the disciples and the Lord
that Thursday evening after sunset. The Gospels make it clear
that when they saw a man carrying a jug on his head, they were
to request the man to prepare a room and the meal (Mark 14:13–
15). Like the owner of the donkey that he rode on Monday during
the Triumphal Entry, this man was probably already a follower of
Jesus and was probably anticipating such a request. Perhaps Jesus had previously asked him during one of his visits to the city if

Figure 9: The traditional site of the Upper Room and Last Supper. Buildings on the site have been destroyed and rebuilt since at least the fourth century.

he could perform a service for him someday. The man then showed them a large upper room and the preparations for the meal and observance began. This would involve a thorough purging of the house from all leaven (*hametz*) and possibly a ceremonial sweeping up of the final breadcrumbs and burning them, as is done today in many Jewish households. Meanwhile, one disciple would have then carried the lamb and stood in a long line in the Temple leading through the Court of the Women into the Court of Israel where he would have handed it over to be killed before quickly returning to the home, probably on the current Mount Zion outside the 16th century Turkish walls.

The Biblical prescription for killing the lamb was that it should take place in the evening or "twilight" (Exod 12:6). The Hebrew is literally "between the evenings." This was interpreted by the rabbis as that period when the sun began to set and when it finished setting. At this point, however, is the problem. Since this slaying was to take place in Jerusalem, and since Jerusalem was filled with thousands upon thousands of Jewish families, each with a lamb, how could this be accomplished during "twilight"? The solution was that a space of around six hours was marked out as the period "between the evenings"—roughly from noon to six p.m.—that larger period was viewed as when the sun began going down and when it finally set.

So one of the disciples carried that lamb which would be consumed by the Lord and his disciples and stood in line, maybe for hours, returning in haste to the house where the mother of the home roasted it whole and prepared the other food including the unleavened bread (*matza*) and the bitter herbs (*maror*), as required by the Torah (Exod 12:8). The ceremony of putting the blood on the lintel and doorposts of each house (12:7, 22) was not repeated each year, since that act was only intended for the original Passover night in Egypt. Oftentimes it is thought that the word *Passover* was meant to describe how the Lord in some way "jumped over" each house, thus sparing the inhabitants from being killed by him. The Biblical text, however, is clear that the image was the Lord passing *over* each house to cover and protect it, not passing *by* it. The protection was to prevent the *destroyer* angel from killing the first born. This is clearly declared in Exodus 12:23 and described poetically later in Psalm 78:49.

The scene at this "Last Supper," as it has come to be called, is indelibly impressed on all of our minds by the many artistic renderings of the scene. The most famous of these is undoubtedly the fresco painting by Leonardo da Vinci on that convent wall in Milan, Italy. I certainly cannot evaluate the quality of that genius in his artistic rendering of the moment when Jesus announced that one of them would deny him. The astonished looks on their faces clearly communicate the question, "Is it I?"

But the scene just did not resemble the painting. Jews, as well as other Romans and Greeks, did not sit around a table like the one in the painting. They reclined on their left elbow at a low table. This is even reflected in the Greek word used for sitting at a table, which literally means "recline" (*anaklino*). Some think the table was called a *triclinium* and had three sides in a sort of squared u-shape, with a space between the sides. I do not think we can be dogmatic, but certainly a low table was used. This also helps us to understand the reference to John being in the breast of Jesus. Too many artists, not understanding this eating custom, have a youthful, often effeminate looking John somehow leaning into Jesus' chest, usually in some strange contortion. When we understand that John was reclining next to Jesus on his left elbow, it is easier to envision how he was "in" Jesus' breast – and someone else, possibly Peter, was also in John's breast. This also helps to explain why Peter was easily able to request John to inquire of Jesus the identity of the betrayer. It also explains that Judas was on the other side of Jesus (who was in his breast) because they could easily put their right hands in a dish at the same time.

A number of possible foods were on that table, but the rabbis said three elements were absolutely essential. Those were the lamb, the bitter herbs, and the *matza*, reflecting the foods that are mentioned in Exodus 12. There is a world of wonderful truths associated with these foods, but this chapter is focusing on matters that are not often known to most Christian readers. Prayers and Scripture readings comprised the text that was read and recited, and today that booklet is called a *Haggadah*. Four cups of wine are drunk, two before the meal itself and two afterward. Each cup is given a name and the third cup, the one taken right after the meal, is called the Cup of Redemption. How appropriate that Jesus took that cup—already signifying redemption—and gave it a new meaning, namely that it represented his blood shed for the "redemption" of our sins! The broken bread symbolized his body broken for us. There is a custom in the Seder meal that goes back to ancient times, namely that one piece of that matza is wrapped and hidden away until after the meal when it is found, unwrapped, and partaken of by all. It is called the *afikomen*, the only Greek word in the *Seder*, and it means either "the coming one" or "I came." I even know of a Jewish author who agrees with the messianic interpretation of the *afikomen*, namely that it refers to the drama of the coming Messiah! It is a beautiful illustration to us that the Messiah was broken, buried, resurrected, and partaken of by his followers!

But where does the provocative title of my chapter come from, namely "Singing for Your Supper?" The ancient Psalms were sung by Israelites, and many Jews and Christians sing them even today. We know what psalms were—and still today—are read and chanted during the Passover Seder. They are the "Hallel Psalms," numbered 113–118. The first three of those Psalms are read before the meal. The last three are read and sung at the conclusion of the Seder. When Matthew informs us that the group, now without Judas, sang a hymn and departed for the Mount of Olives, one might wonder what they sang. Well, it was not "Blessed Be the Tie That Binds!" We actually know what *hymn* they sang. It was Psalms 116–118. Now please notice the last words of Psalm 118:

> I thank you that you have answered me
> and have become my salvation.
> **The stone that the builders rejected**
> **has become the cornerstone.**
> This is the LORD's doing; it is marvelous in our eyes.
> **This is the day that the LORD has made;**
> **let us rejoice and be glad in it.**
> Save us, we pray, O LORD!
> O LORD, we pray, give us success!
> **Blessed is he who comes in the name of the LORD!**
> We bless you from the house of the LORD (Ps 118:21–26).

These were the last words on the lips of the Lord Jesus before he departed for Gethsemane and ultimately Golgotha. The Messiah who had been rejected sang about the stone which the builders rejected (Ps 118:22a)! Jesus had already quoted and applied that text at the end of the most transparent parable he had ever told on Wednesday morning, just before he went dark, weeping over that rejection (Matt 21:42). And yet the day of his rejection was the day his Father appointed him as the cornerstone in a new temple (Ps 118:22b), and this was a day which the Lord made and over which he and his followers could rejoice (118:24). Jesus then sings about the blessing on the one who comes in the name of the Lord (118:26). I remind the reader that this text was shouted out during the Triumphal Entry (Matt 21:9), and he solemnly prophesied that Israel would not see him publicly until they joined in this messianic pronouncement on him (Matt 23:39).

Therefore, Psalm 118 appears during the Passion Week no less than four times in a messianic role. Three times the words of this psalm explicitly appear in the texts and events mentioned above, and once implicitly in the hymn that Jesus and his disciples sang before they went out to Gethsemane and to the passion of suffering that lay ahead for him. While it is often affirmed that Psalm 110 is the most cited OT passage by NT writers, Psalm 118, with all its allusions, is a very close second. Yet how few Bible readers recognize that fact!

Yes, Jesus and the eleven that were left were "singing for their supper" and it was a sober song about rejection. That song, however, ended on a triumphant note because the day of the rejected stone became for Jesus the day of his installation as the cornerstone. Let us sing that song with him!*

---

*For further information on Passover and other Jewish observances, see Steven Herzig, *Jewish Culture and Customs: A Sampler of Jewish Life* (Friends of Israel, 1997).

Suggested Prayer: "Lord Jesus, I take communion so often, and I confess that sometimes it becomes simply a ritual. As you commanded us to do this in your remembrance, may I always remember that the sacrifice of your blood and your body took place so I could be forgiven and have communion with you. I love you, Lord, because you first loved me."

Figure 10: Stairs from antiquity that may have been used by Jesus to go from the Last Supper to Gethsemane.

7

No "Garden of Gethsemane!"
Is Nothing Sacred?

Matthew says it simply, "And when they had sung a hymn, they went out to the Mount of Olives" (Matt 26:30). But where did they go on the Mount of Olives? If you ask that question to a group of Christians, you will receive an almost universal response: "Why the Garden of Gethsemane, of course!" But none of the Gospels answer the question with that expression. Matthew records it the way Mark and Luke do. "Then Jesus went with them to a place called Gethsemane" (Matt 26:36; see also Mark 14:32). While Luke does not use that title for the place, he adds something important, "And he came out and went, as was his custom, to the Mount of Olives, and the disciples followed him" (Luke 22:39). John mentions that it was across the Kidron Valley, east of the city (John 18:1). From these texts we learn the place to which Jesus took the eleven was where he had taken them at least on the previous night, that is, Wednesday. As we will see, this habit of Jesus was known to Judas since he had slept there the previous night, so he knew where he could deliver Jesus to the religious authorities without a big crowd around which would have prevented his traitorous deed. The authorities had actually given up on capturing Jesus within the next week. "Then the chief priests and the elders of the people gathered in the palace of the high priest, whose name was Caiaphas, and plotted together in order to arrest Jesus by stealth and kill him. But they said, 'Not during the feast, lest there be an uproar among the people'" (Matt 26:3–5).

Before we explore further this deed of Judas, what motivated him, and see how they captured Jesus, let's look a little closer at this special place and what it was actually called. Here is the shocker to some. There is no reference to the expression "Garden of Gethsemane" in the Synoptics. John does mention a nearby garden (18:1), but even he does not use the expression "Garden of Gethsemane." It is simply referred to as "Gethsemane." The word is a transliteration of the Aramaic expression *Gat Shemen*, which means "oil-press." Today there is a cave at the base of the Mount of Olives, next to the traditional Tomb of the Virgin, and less than a hundred yards from the traditional "Garden of Gethsemane" which is on the grounds of the Church of All Nations. Scholars believe that it is one of the most reliable locations for an event mentioned in the Gospels. This cave would be a perfect spot for Jesus and the twelve to camp out during the Passover week. You could keep reasonably warm there and be protected from the elements. There is even a notch in the wall that held the end of the beam of an olive press. The cave is right next to a grove of ancient olive trees, and the owner of that olive grove pressed his olives into oil in that cave. The olive harvest comes in the fall, so in the spring, the owner wasn't using his cave and may well have rented it out to visitors for the Passover. The cave is about 60 feet long and 36 feet wide and could easily have held more than a dozen people. Here Jesus would also be safe from the prying eyes of the authorities—unless one of his friends ratted on him—which is

Figure 11: The Gethsemane Cave would have offered refuge for Jesus and his disciples.

exactly what happened! The reason you can visit the cave today is because there is a long tradition (going back to at least the fourth century) that this was the site of the arrest of Jesus. The Franciscans later built a very simple chapel in the cave, and you can see stars painted in ancient times on the ceiling of the cave that recall the nighttime prayers of Jesus in this area. I have taken

hundreds of my students to this cave and many have expressed
that it was the spiritual highlight of their trip.

Jesus faced the most difficult temptation of his earthly life
during his agony in the area of Gethsemane. Earlier, in the face of
Satan's temptations in the wilderness, when he was at his greatest physical weakness, he firmly responded with Scripture to silence the tempter (Matt 4:1–11). Here in Gethsemane was a
greater weakness than lack of food – the agony of facing a hor-
rendous death by bearing a world of sins – that caused him to ask
his Father to take away the cup he was being asked to drink. It
was the cup appointed for him, much as the psalmist spoke pos-
itively about the cup assigned to him (Ps 23:3). Jesus knew that
his Father was asking him to do this, but the horror of it all led
him to ask his Father to take it all away! In the end he yielded to
his Father's will. Could the Savior have sinned? Such a thought
causes some to recoil at even the idea that the sinless Son of God
could ever sin, but isn't the possibility of sinning part of his real
humanity? We evangelicals confess both the true deity and the
true humanity of Jesus. The fact remains that he did *not* sin, so
some will think it is useless to speculate on what theologians call
the impeccability or peccability of the Savior. For years I argued
firmly for his impeccability (that he was not able to sin), but my
study of the Letter to the Hebrews has challenged me to
acknowledge that he could have sinned (peccability), but he did
not. That fact in Gethsemane, coupled with his earlier victory
over temptation in the wilderness, enables me to appreciate even
more how he can really help me as my high priest when I come
boldly to his present throne of grace. See if you agree that the Savior's help means so much more as he moved from peccability to
perfection at this stage in his ministry, so graphically described
in Hebrews. "In the days of his flesh, Jesus offered up prayers and
supplications, with *loud cries and tears*, to him who was able to

save him from death, and he was heard because of his reverence. Although he was a son, he learned obedience through what he suffered. And being made perfect, he became the source of eternal salvation to all who obey him, being designated by God a high priest after the order of Melchizedek" (Heb 5:7–10). There was a sense that he was not complete before he became complete, and until that *perfection* he could have sinned. But he passed the ultimate test! That is why he can sympathize with our weaknesses and provide us with real help—because he was tempted in all points as we are—yet without sin! (Heb 4:4:14–15). His ability to sin, but his refusal to do so makes me appreciate his overcoming temptation even more. A new appreciation of his true humanity awaits those who recognize this.

As Jesus passes this temptation, the dirty deed of Judas can then be done, and without that huge crowd around Jesus to protect him! The betrayer had made the deal and led the Sanhedrin leaders there with their officers under darkness of night. What, therefore, can we say about this miserable man? The Gospels are clear that Judas was the treasurer of this group but allowed the love of that money to control him at times. But I believe that his avarice is just too simple an explanation for what he did. If he simply wanted those 30 coins, why then did he throw them back to the Temple authorities when he saw Jesus arrested? In my opinion there was something more complex going on in this man's mind than simple greed. Here is my controversial proposal: Judas shared with his fellow disciples a belief that was actually held by all of them to the end. It had to do with the *how* of bringing in the kingdom, involving the overthrow of the Romans, by force if necessary—and it would have been very necessary! Peter even drew his sword and tried to stop the arrest (John 18:10–11). They thought that the outward and physical kingdom could be brought in, but Jesus in that garden (yes there was one nearby, John 18:1) even told them that if they fought for this kingdom, how could the suffering prophecies be fulfilled (John 18:11; Matt 26:53–54)? I think that Judas, seeing the public acclamation of Jesus in the Triumphal Entry, thought that he would be something like the Secretary of the Treasury in this new "kingdom." But in the following days he became disillusioned when that so-called Triumphal Entry did not result in an anti-Roman revolution but actually led to Jesus teaching something else about his rejection and suffering. I think that Judas then tried to push the Savior's hand to violently resist this arrest. When Jesus, however, rather submitted to the chains, he knew it was all a waste, and he threw the money back into the Temple and hanged himself. Some may say that I am trying to lessen Judas' guilt and deny his avarice. Absolutely not! It was his avarice that pushed him over the top, something that the rest of Jesus' very disappointed disciples did not do (Luke 24:19–21)! Throwing the money back to the bribers did not remove his guilt so he then paid the ultimate price with his own life.

At the end of the Gethsemane drama, Mark alone records a rather strange event. When his disciples fled at Jesus' arrest there was a young "streaker" watching in the bushes who also fled "naked" as his garment was grabbed from him (14:50–51). The lack of a mentioned name for this young man has led to many suggestions about his identity, possibly John or James or even young Mark himself, recording for us a self-effacing *signature* to his Gospel. The Mark identity is supported not only by the Markan authorship of the Gospel, but also by the fact that the early church met in the house of John Mark's mother (Acts 12) and the probability that her house was also the location of the Last Supper. In other words, the young man may have been watching the Seder from his room and then rushed out without being fully clothed as they left for Gethsemane. I think this is the best possible suggestion for his identity, with "protective anonymity" as a motive for the Gospel's silence about his identity. Perhaps, however, too much speculation about his identity is misplaced. What does Mark want us to see in this incident in light of his whole Gospel? Certainly his fleeing (14:50–51) was meant to be seen as parallel to the larger fleeing of the disciples just mentioned (14:49). But is there still more?

Within Mark there are two possible intratextual connections with this strange event. Note that in Mark 14:51 there is a young man (*neaniskos*) clothed (*peribeblemonon*) in a garment (*sindonon*). Later in the empty tomb description (16:5) there is a young man (*neaniskos*) clothed (*peribeblemonon*) in a robe (*stolen*). Is this intended by Mark to contrast the fear and naked abandonment of the young man in Gethsemane with the victorious and clothed announcement of another young man in the tomb? The fact that Mark alone calls the tomb angel a "young man" certainly makes his intentional association of these two incidents a real possibility.

There is, however, an earlier Markan text that may be an even closer comparison and contrast with 15:40–41. In the account of the healing of blind Bartimaeus (10:46–52), the healed man casts off his garment and runs to Jesus (10:50). Although the language utilizes synonyms rather than the exact words of 15:40–41, the contrast between the accounts is powerfully made. The emotion of the two episodes may be different, but the function of the shedding of the garment is essentially the same, and why even mention Bartimaeus' casting off his garment? The Bartimaeus episode also comes at the pinnacle of events leading up to the Passion week, and the blind man is described as following Jesus, an event that issues in a joyous discipleship that accepts the earlier passion as the way to the cross. On the other hand, the naked youth represents an abortive attempt at discipleship but ends in a humiliating flight. The evidence of the shed garment in both accounts (chs 10 and 14) may be even stronger than the shared words in the last two accounts (chs 14 and 16). Perhaps Mark, however, would be surprised that we should want to choose between the best parallel account in chapters 10 and 16. He may have intended that we see both the recovered Bartimaeus and the young man in the tomb as each pointing first forward and then backward to this incident in Gethsemane that only he recorded.*

No one more than me recognizes that there is much more to the Gethsemane events than what has been mentioned. I hope that these fresh looks at some familiar texts will give us a deeper appreciation for what went on during that momentous night in the olive oil cave and among the olive trees.

———————▼———————

*See Abraham Kuruvilla, "The Naked Runaway and the Enrobed Reporter of Mark 14 and 16: What is the Author Doing with What He Is Saying?" *JETS*, 54.3 (September 2011), 527–45.

Suggested Prayer: "Lord Jesus, as I naturally shrink from the tasks that I must do, I am reminded that in your true humanity you did not want to follow that path that was determined by your Father. I need the same grace that was given to you to face the hard path ahead. Help me by your grace (Heb 4:16) in my own time of need to not seek my will but the will of my Father, even if it means a hard road ahead. Lord Jesus your grace is sufficient for me."

8

JESUS BARABBAS OR JESUS MESSIAH?
THOSE "FICKLE" JEWS!

T hen Jesus headed back, retracing his earlier steps, although this time he was not with his disciples but with an armed guard and some religious leaders. They crossed back over the Kidron Valley, over and through a hill that was the oldest part of Jerusalem, crossed the Central Valley (called the Cheesemakers Valley by Josephus), then ascended the western hill of the city, known today as Mt Zion. It was on this hill that Jesus would spend the next twelve hours of his earthly life, being eventually condemned to a cruel death by both Jewish and Roman leaders.

Not everything in this book is new or fresh or controversial. It is agreed by all that during the night and early morning, Jesus went through two series of three trials. Of course the word *trial* should not raise any mental images of what we think of today as a trial. These were more like hearings, since the guilt of Jesus had already been decided by the Jewish religious leaders. First were the three Jewish trials: (1) before Annas, the father in law of the high priest, Caiaphas; (2) before Caiaphas himself; and (3) before the Sanhedrin or at least a part of that body. Then came the Roman trials: (1) before Pilate; (2) before Herod Antipas; and (3) before Pilate again.

We will focus on the following issues, which I believe can be enlightened by some fresh insights.

1. The numerous violations of Jewish courtroom and legal practices that took place in the three Jewish trials.
2. The dramatic final scene between Jesus and Caiaphas and the astounding claim that was made by Jesus.
3. The strange encounter with Herod Antipas.
4. The actions surrounding Barabbas.
5. The charge heard from many that the Jerusalem Jews were "fickle" in radically changing their attitude on Monday to their opposite attitude on Friday.

The rabbis have left us a fascinating description of Jewish legal regulations in a tractate of the Mishna called *Sanhedrin*. It describes in detail how trials were to be conducted. When one examines those regulations, it is clearly seen that nearly two dozen of the rules and regulations for Jewish trials were violated in the trials of Jesus. We will mention only a few but enough to recognize that the Jewish trials of Jesus were actually illegal according to their own standards. For example, trying Jesus at night violated the Mishnaic law that *there were to be no trials before the morning sacrifice.* John 18:19–22 indicates that the trial was held in secret, violating the Mishnaic law that *there were to be no secret trials, only public ones.* Luke 22:54 states that the Sanhedrin gathered in the high priest's house, thus violating the Mishnaic law that *Sanhedrin trials could only be conducted in the Hall of Judgment in the Temple.* Matthew 26:59 states that the trial began with the religious leaders seeking false witnesses against Jesus. This broke the Mishnaic law that *the defense was to have the first word before any prosecutors could present their accusations.* Mark 14:55 states that the entire council acted in unison against Jesus, breaking the

Mishnaic law that *all could vote for acquittal, but not all could vote for conviction.*

Matthew 26:61 and Mark 14:58–59 state that the witnesses clearly contradicted each other in reporting Jesus' statements regarding the Temple. This broke the Mishnaic law that *there must be two or three witnesses and that they must agree on every detail.* This disqualified the witnesses so Jesus should have been released at that point. According to Matthew 26:65, Caiaphas introduced the charge of blasphemy, thus breaking the Mishnaic law that *judges could not initiate the charges but could only investigate charges that were brought to them.* The charge was blasphemy but then Caiaphas also broke another Mishnaic law that *blasphemy only took place if the four letter name of God (Yahweh) was pronounced.* As we will see, that was not the case when Jesus cited Daniel 7 and Psalm 110. As a follow up to this last action, Caiaphas' condemnation of Jesus' claim also broke the Mishnaic law that *a person could not be condemned on the basis of his words alone.*

Getting tired? Remember that I am being selective on the breaking of these Mishnaic laws. Just a few more! The condemnation of Jesus took place while it was still night, which broke the Mishnaic law that in cases of capital punishment the verdict could not be announced at night, as well as the Mishnaic law that *the trial and verdict could not occur at the same time, but had to be separated by at least a day.* There was no reference to voting on Jesus' condemnation which also broke the Mishnaic law that *the death penalty had to be done by individual count from the youngest to the eldest.* In announcing the guilty verdict immediately, the Mishnaic law was broken that *the sentence could only be pronounced three days after the guilty verdict.* As if this was not enough to illustrate the corrupt administration of Caiaphas, the event took place between the first and second nights of Passover.

This broke the Mishnaic law that no trials were allowed on the eve of the Sabbath or of a Jewish holiday. And where were Nicodemus and Joseph of Arimathea during this charade? Maybe they were not even notified and were not present since it was probably known that they were sympathetic to this Galilean.*

I realize that the past two paragraphs have been rather tedious reading, but I again remind the patient reader that I have been selective in the Mishnaic laws that were broken in the Jewish *trial* of Jesus. John 11:49–53 indicates that Caiaphas wanted above all to protect his own privileged position, so nothing would stop him and his sympathizers from getting rid of this troublemaker. The corruption of the priesthood was another reason that the Book of Hebrews saw the need for another high priest to arise, even if he is in a different kind of priesthood, superior to the Levitical one (Hebrews 7).

We cannot leave this sad scene without mentioning the theological high point at the culmination of this so-called trial. Matthew portrays it dramatically: "But Jesus remained silent. And the high priest said to him, 'I adjure you by the living God, tell us if you are the Christ, the Son of God.' Jesus said to him, 'You have said so. But I tell you, from now on you will see the Son of Man seated at the right hand of Power and coming on the clouds of heaven.' Then the high priest tore his robes and said, 'He has uttered blasphemy. What further witnesses do we need? You have now heard his blasphemy'" (Matt 26:63–65). Modern readers may misunderstand Jesus' response to Caiaphas' straightforward question as being a sort of dodge, like responding: "Well that is what you are saying, but..." Not so, because this was actually a way in ancient times of saying "yes" to a question. In any case, Mark's account makes the positive affirmation of Jesus quite clear (Mark 14:62). As evidence that Jesus was affirming Caiaphas' question was the high priest's definitive response that Jesus claimed to be the heavenly Son of Man in Daniel 7:13 and the Lord at the Lord's right hand in Psalm 110:1. He tore his robes as a sign of mourning over Jesus' "blasphemy" (see Mark 14:63).

Michael Bird offers a telling observation on the importance of this passage. "Jesus' claim is not that he's going to sit on his own little throne next to God; rather, he will sit at God's right hand on God's throne. If Jesus thinks that Dan 7:13 –14 is about him, then he is placing himself within the orbit of divine sovereignty and claiming a place within the divine regency of God Almighty. If he's wrong, it isn't just bad theology; it is blasphemy and an affront to Jewish monotheism."** The reader should pause and reflect on these passages and recognize the enormity of his claim, a claim not recognized by unitarians who deny that Jesus was the heavenly and Divine Messiah. I find it interesting that the unbelieving Caiaphas *got it* even if modern cultists refuse to see it!

The *Roman* trial remained, because Caiaphas knew that capital punishment for such a *crime* was not permitted to them, since the Romans had taken away from the Sanhedrin the *lex gladii* (law of the sword). Only the Roman procurator could condemn Jesus to death and then carry it out. Caiaphas knew, however, that Pilate would not be interested in some Jewish fuss about blasphemy, so he sent Jesus to him with the rather absurd charge of sedition and rebellion against Roman rule. After a brief interview with Jesus, Pilate saw that the man before him was no zealot nor inciter to violence. Upon learning that Jesus was from Galilee, he thought he could get rid of the problem and sent him over to Herod Antipas who was in Jerusalem for Passover (Luke 23:7–12).

Antipas was the son and successor of Herod the Great, and like his father, his Jewishness was suspect but reluctantly acknowledged by his subjects. Keep in mind that this is the same Herod who was tormented by another prophet whom we know as John the Baptist. It is ironic that a party was involved in both of these encounters with Antipas (see Mark 6:21–27). At that party, Antipas fell for the trick from his adulterous wife and daughter, and it all lead to John's beheading. Antipas was not going to fall again for this ruse, so he asked Jesus to entertain his friends by doing a *miracle*, much like a birthday boy would have a magician entertain his friends at his party. At this point the reader may be surprised if I introduce an example from the often-blasphemous rock opera "Jesus Christ Superstar" to illustrate this scene. But stay with me and try to see my point. Contemporary rock is the normal music for that opera up to this point, but here Andrew Lloyd Webber switches to a *rag time* tune, and the following words are addressed by Antipas to a silent Jesus. "So you are the Christ, you're the great Jesus Christ, show to me that you're no fool—walk across my swimming pool!" Whatever one thinks about the rest of the musical, I think the composer nailed it here by putting this shallow song in the mouth of an equally shallow Herod Antipas. He was not interested in truth; he was interested only in a magic trick. But Jesus did not come to perform tricks to satisfy the shallow curiosity of party-goers. So he simply remained silent (Luke 23:9).

I wonder what went through Pilate's mind when Jesus was led back to him? "Oh, no, not him again! How do I get rid of him?" He knew Jesus was innocent and even his wife warned him about that (Matt 27:19). Then it hit him. "Oh, wait a minute, don't these Jews have a custom of my releasing a prisoner in the place of another?" That brings us back to the drama of Barabbas, or should I call him "Jesus Barabbas?" Barabbas was not just a *thief*; he was an armed bandit, a revolutionary who had murdered and who was about to be executed. Pilate capitalized on this custom and thought he could get rid of Jesus. Certainly the crowd would choose Jesus over this notorious bad boy! There was a great irony in this putting forth of the choice between Barabbas and Jesus.

Figure 12: The ossuary that once contained the bones of Caiaphas, the high priest who condemned Jesus. Israel Museum.

The irony was that "Barabbas" was not his proper name but was a reference to his father. It is a Greek transliteration of the Aramaic word *bar*, meaning "son" and *Abba* which was his father's name. This would make him "Son of Abba." There is some interesting evidence that his given name was *Jesus* (or *Yeshua* in Aramaic). The name "Jesus Barabbas" is preserved in a 9th century Greek codex of the Gospels as well as in some earlier Syriac manuscripts. Not only that, but the third century Church Father, Origen, mentioned that there were other ancient Greek manuscripts that preserved this reading of his full name. I personally think this was the original reading in Matthew and scribes just could not stomach the idea that this awful man shared the same given name as Jesus of Nazareth and began to omit it in the scribal tradition of copies.

If this is an accurate assessment, look at the ironies involved. Two men shared the same name, Jesus, while one was guilty of the crime of sedition and the other was accused but innocent of the crime of sedition! A further irony is that Barabbas' father's name was *Abba* which means a "father" on earth. Jesus was also truly the son of the "Father" in heaven. A respected English version like the NIV even adopts this quite dramatic and ironic translation. "So when the crowd had gathered, Pilate asked them, 'Which one do you want me to release to you: Jesus Barabbas, or Jesus who is called the Messiah?'" (Matt 27:17).

The choice was clear, but Matthew says that the chief priests and elders did not want to allow any opportunity for Jesus of Nazareth to be released. Their action is one of the most overlooked foul deeds in this scenario, and it will form the basis of our last fresh insight into what, in my opinion, is one of the most serious misreadings of the Passion Week. Pilate's wife entered the scene with her warning (Matt 27:19) which provided a long enough interruption for the following to take place. Here is the plain statement of Matt 27:20: "Now the chief priests and the elders persuaded the crowd to ask for Barabbas and destroy Jesus." Why do I consider this as one of the most overlooked facts in the week? It has to do with something that I have heard over and over from preachers and teachers who should know better. It goes something like this. "How fickle those Jews were! They shifted from hailing him as Messiah on Monday during the Triumphal Entry and then four days later they are calling for his blood" (27:23–25). If I can only put one lie to death in this book, I want to end this awful canard and unscriptural accusation.

There are two reasons I am immensely serious about this problem. The first is that this charge breathes a latent but serious anti-Semitism in its slander against the Jewish people as a whole. In other words, they not only were fickle but they also were collectively guilty of Jesus' murder! The sad thing is that many who mouth these things do not realize how awful a charge against the Jews they are making. Because of their ignorance, I can forgive them for that. The second reason, however, is harder to simply overlook as another interpretation. It is because it is simply unscriptural. Let the words of the great A. T. Robertson focus our attention on the answer to this question. In his *Word Pictures in the New Testament*, he writes on Mark 15:11: "If one wonders why the crowd was fickle, recall that *this was not the crowd* that followed him in the Triumphal Entry and in the Temple. That was the plan—to get the thing over before the Galilean sympathizers woke up."

I should quote that verse from Matt 27:20 again! "Now the chief priests and the elders *persuaded the crowd* to ask for Barabbas and destroy Jesus." This was not the crowd which welcomed him a few days before! That crowd continued to follow Jesus through the week! It astounds me at times when I hear teachers totally ignoring the statements in the Gospels that "the common people heard him gladly" throughout the week (Mark 12:37). How many times do the Gospels have to say that the religious leaders could not get at Jesus because these common people were protecting him? See the earlier chapter, "How Did Jesus Get Away with Cleansing the Temple?" Check out again Matt 21:46: "They looked for a way to arrest him, but they were afraid of the crowd because *the people held that he was a prophet.*" This motley crowd that gathered early Friday in the Praetorium was not that large group that was eager to follow Jesus from Monday through Wednesday. There is absolutely no evidence that this was the same crowd. My guess is that most of the Jesus followers were just waking up. Even the eleven were somewhere in fear since they all fled from Gethsemane. Please, my readers, let us put this lie to rest forever! It is simply unscriptural at the worst and latently anti-semitic at the best. It is a shame that events as important as the passion of our Lord could be marred by such sadly perpetuated ideas.

———————▼———————

*Thanks to Arnold G. Fruchtenbaum for ideas on the Jewish "trials" adapted from his *Yeshua: The Life of Messiah from a Messianic Jewish Perspective*, 2nd ed. (Ariel Ministries, 2018).

**Bird's quotation is from a valuable volume exploring the passages that argue for Jesus' deity: Michael Bird, ed., *How God Became Jesus: The Real Origins of Belief in Jesus' Divine Nature—A Response to Bart Ehrman* (Zondervan, 2016).

Suggested prayer: "Lord Jesus, how unjustly did unjust people treat you! How silent you were in the place of false charges about what you said and did! Lord, if someone else treats me unfairly, help me again to recognize how unfairly and unjustly you endured such charges without any sinful response. Oh, Lord, you suffered, the just one for unjust people like me. May I never complain when suffering some small insult when you endured silently all that you did for me!"

Figure 13: The Western Wall of the Temple is a focus of devotion for Jewish crowds. In Jesus' day, crowds followed him, but others were stirred up against him by a few powerful leaders.

9

There Was No "Mount" Calvary!
Who Was Forsaken and What Was Finished?

This is a familiar road for any believer—Gethsemane, Trials, Crucifixion. The passion of Jesus reaches its finale after his carrying a cross to the site of his crucifixion. But what was that place called? The Gospels make that answer very clear but subsequent years have added a noun to that place, "Hill of Calvary" or "Mount Calvary." That last title has become part of the name of many an evangelical church! This chapter will suggest the following denials that go against the grain of traditional readings of this precious series of events: (1) there was no "Mount Calvary"; (2) the Father did not forsake the Son at the crucifixion; and (3) redemption was not "finished" upon his death.

I know those statements may be surprising and even shocking to many readers, but let us look at the evidence. There is no reference anywhere in the New Testament that the site of Jesus' crucifixion was on a "mount" or "hill" of any sort. One word is used for the site and that word is "Golgotha" (Matt 27:33; Mark 15:22; John 19:17), which is the Aramaic word for "skull." Those three writers translate this word with the Greek expression *kraniou topos* or "skull place." So where did our word "Calvary" come from? The Latin Vulgate translates the Greek "place of the skull" as *Calvariae locus.* The Latin word for "Calvary" means "skull." So our word "Calvary" comes from the Latin phrase "place of the skull (*Calvariae*)," which itself is a translation of the Gospel's Aramaic phrase Golgotha ("skull") that described the location of Jesus' crucifixion.

I emphasize again that nowhere in the Greek New Testament or in its Latin translation is there any mention of a "Hill called Mount Calvary," although it is celebrated as such in many a Gospel song and artistic rendition. It is difficult to uncover how the tradition of it being a hill actually arose. Perhaps it entered hymnody through its wrong identification by General Gordon who thought that the rocky edge of an old quarry north of Jerusalem was "Skull Hill." There is no need for the place of execution to be on a hill since being beside a main thoroughfare into a western gate of Jerusalem provided enough visibility to passersby to see it and mock (John 19:20; Heb 13:12). The most reliable location today for Golgotha is the Church of the Holy Sepulcher and no hill is there. The two small chapels of Calvary are on top of an old stone outcropping, which in no way is anything like a hill. Why was it called "Skull?" Either because it was a place of death and/or, as John 19:41 tell us, because it served also as a cemetery.

The second denial in this chapter will be more controversial. The Father did not forsake the Son on the cross. Jesus uttered at least seven sayings or *last words* on the cross. One of the first is recorded in Aramaic "*Eloi, Eloi, lemá sabachtháni?*" (Mark 15:34). Matthew records the Hebrew "Eli Eli" (27:46). The translation is given by the writers, "My God, my God, why have you forsaken (or abandoned) me?" With such a clear statement as this, how could I even suggest that the Father did not forsake his Son at Calvary?

To answer that question we must look at the source of Jesus' cry and its meaning in its context. Everyone agrees that the source of this "cry of dereliction," as it is often called, is Psalm 22:1. No, I am not going to claim that our translations are bad. That is exactly what the Hebrew says. Evangelicals live and die by the maxim, "Context is king." Sometimes we use the saying, "A text without a context can become a pretext." That last saying is certainly the case here. Assuming that the Father *did* abandon his Son has led to many homiletical explanations that raise all sort of theological issues. How could the Father forsake his Son with whom he shared intimacy and communion? How could such a disjunct take place within the Godhead?

The usual answer is that when the Son bore the sins of mankind, the Father could not look upon him in that sinful condition, because he cannot look upon sin. There are two problems with that. The first is that such an explanation is read into the verse. It does not state that either in the OT or in the Gospels. The second problem is that God looks upon sin all the time. He is omniscient and all seeing. He does not approve of sin, but he is very aware of it and sees it. Such explanations are faulty and are simply not needed when we see Psalm 22:1 in its original setting. So what exactly is that setting?

Psalm 22 is a psalm in which the psalmist laments before the Lord regarding his condition and/or situation. For other individual laments, see Psalms 3, 39, 57, 139. You know you are reading a Lament Psalm when early on you read the words "Why" or "How long?" Some of these laments can get pretty heavy and pessimistic and negative. Because of this, it is important to look for what I call the *pivot*, when the psalmist turns from a pessimistic lament to trust and even praise. Psalm 22 contains lament, a pivot, and even praise.

The psalm is all over the accounts of the passion. It is the most quoted, cited, and alluded to Old Testament text in these passages, with Isaiah 53 and Psalm 118 coming in as close seconds.

Because it is mentioned so many times, I am convinced that when Jesus takes the words of Psalm 22 on his own lips, he is evoking the entire psalm as descriptive of his experience. Therefore, we should look at the entire psalm as describing what he was going through, and when we do that, we come to the following conclusions.

This psalm, although beginning as a lament, emerges as a psalm describing his vindication and victory! The pivot comes around verse 21. After a fervent prayer to be delivered from all these animals that serve figuratively as representing his persecutors (vv. 12–21a), he cries out: "You have rescued me from the horns of the wild oxen! I will tell of your name to my brothers; in the midst of the congregation I will praise you… For he has not despised or abhorred the affliction of the afflicted, and **he has not hidden his face from him**, but has heard, when he cried to him" (vv. 21b–24). I have bolded the words that indicate that the Father did not abandon the Son. Furthermore, a verse from this passage (v. 22) is actually quoted in Hebrews 2:12 as the words of the victorious and resurrected Jesus speaking in the midst of the NT church! So what appeared to Jesus in the midst of his human suffering as abandonment eventually issued as a victory cry. This can even be seen in some of the subsequent sayings of Jesus on the cross such as, "Today you will be with me in paradise," and, "Into your hands I commit my spirit." The crowning words of the psalm in 22:31, "he has done it," are echoed in the parting cry "it is finished," which we will soon consider. Therefore, in light of the entire lament psalm, the Father did not forsake his Son.

The third *denial* (although I don't like that negative word) that I wish to declare is that Jesus' work of atoning for our sins is not what John 19:30, "it is finished," is all about. I suggest another approach to the famous last word of Jesus in John 19:30—*tetelestai* —usually translated as "it is finished." In the context of John 19, it refers to the finishing of the suffering prophecies (especially Ps 22) rather than the finishing of redemption.

As a matter of fact, the exact word that is used in 19:30 (*tetelestai*) is used two verses earlier in 19:28 of prophecies being fulfilled in Jesus' passion. "After this, Jesus, knowing that all things (plural) were now finished (*tetelestai*), said, that the scripture be fulfilled, 'I thirst.' A jar full of sour wine stood there, so they put a sponge full of the sour wine on a hyssop branch and held it to his mouth" (19:28–29). John uses the same verb in 19:28 in the same form as used by Jesus in 19:30. Because the neuter plural "all things" was used as the subject of *tetelestai* in 19:28, I suggest that the same verb form in 19:30 could also be translated as "they are finished," referring in this context to the prophecies of his suffering.

On the night before, during the Passover Seder, Jesus used this very same verb (*teleo*, from which comes the form *tetelestai*) about the prophecies that would be "finished" in his death. "For I tell you, what is written must be fulfilled (*teleo*) in me: 'And he was counted among the lawless'" (Isa 53:12). "Yes, what is written about me is coming to its fulfillment (*telos*)" (Luke 22:37). What Jesus said would be fulfilled/finished during the Supper was fulfilled/finished on the cross. Finally, that same verb (*teleo*) will also be used by Paul in Acts 13:29, where it again refers to the Scriptures being finished at Jesus' death. "And when they finished (*etelesan*) all the things written about him (i.e., the suffering prophecies), they took him down from the tree and buried him in a tomb." The meaning in Acts 13:29 is the same as here in John 19:30, namely that every essential point in the prophetic portraiture of Messiah was "finished."

The way in which John 19:30 is most often preached can be summed up in the eloquent comments of the eighteenth-century Baptist John Gill, who explained the phrase "it is finished" as follows:

The whole will of God; that he should be incarnate, be exposed
to shame and reproach, and suffer much, and die; the whole
work his Father gave him to do, which was to preach the Gospel,
work miracles, and obtain eternal salvation for his people, all
which were now done, or as good as done; the whole righteous-
ness of the law was fulfilled, and the penalty of death endured;
and redemption from its curse and condemnation secured; sin
was made an end of, full atonement and satisfaction for it were
given; complete pardon procured, peace made, and redemption
from all iniquity obtained; all enemies were conquered; all
types, promises, and prophecies were fulfilled, and his own
course of life ended: the reason of his saying so was, because all
this was near being done, just upon finishing, and was as good
as done; and was sure and certain, and so complete, that nothing need, or could be added to it (*An Exposition of the Gospel According to John,* Newport Commentary Series [Particular Baptist
Press, 2003], 592-93).

I can hear many of my fellow evangelicals crying out a hearty
"amen" when hearing those powerful words. They do convey a
wonderfully robust theology expressed by this great commenta-
tor. But is all of that included in the one word, *tetelestai*? Is it
simply too much weight to lay on John 19:30, especially since the
context does not point to such conclusions? Are we sometimes
guilty of unwittingly reading back onto John 19:30 a later devel-
oped Pauline theology? I suggest that we be satisfied with reading John 19:30 as Jesus' announcing triumphantly that such passages as Psalm 22:1–18 and Isaiah 53:4–12 have been "finished"
and fulfilled in his suffering and death. That is profound enough
in my opinion. In a later chapter, I will suggest that there was a
time when atonement WAS finished. I will develop the idea that
Old Testament atonement was accomplished on *Yom Kippur*
(Day of Atonement) in two stages, first at the altar and then

inside the Holy of Holies. Jesus' atoning work was also in two stages—first on the earthly cross and then in the heavenly temple. This is clearly taught, not only by the analogy with Yom Kippur, but also in that neglected literary masterpiece that we call the Letter to the Hebrews, especially chs. 9 and 10. There we read that after his death at Golgotha, Jesus offered himself in heaven to the Father. That is when atonement was completely "finished." There is more to come when we try to shed some fresh light on the most neglected events of our redemption, the ascension of Jesus where he offered himself to the Father.*

<hr />

*For insights on the use of these OT texts by Jesus and the NT writers, especially the role of Psalm 22, see Stanley Porter, *Sacred Tradition in the New Testament* (Baker, 2019).

Suggested prayer: "Lord Jesus, the apostle Paul cried out, 'God forbid that I should glory except in the cross of my Lord Jesus Christ' (Gal 6:17). The hymn writer wrote: 'Nothing in my hand I bring, simply to thy cross I cling.' It is so easy to forget your suffering, and also to forget that it was for me. During the next time I take the communion bread, may I realize like never before that your body was broken on the cross—for me."

Figure 14: The Church of the Holy Sepulcher was built in a rock quarry outside the city walls, and is almost surely the site of Jesus' burial.

10

WHAT DAY IS IT?

I have spent most of my time up to this point offering alternatives to traditional readings of the events in Passion Week. In this chapter, however, I want to defend a traditional understanding of the events that took place on Friday, the crucifixion and burial of Jesus. But I want to defend the Friday crucifixion with some possibly non-traditional arguments.

While not encountering it very often, occasionally one hears of an effort to reject the traditional Friday crucifixion day in favor of a Wednesday or Thursday date. The evidence for such a change comes down to one main piece of *evidence*—the statement by Jesus in Matthew 12:40 that, just as Jonah was three days and nights in the belly of the fish, so the Son of Man will be three days and nights in the heart of the earth. There is no way, the argument goes, in which the seventy-two hours implied in the expression "three days and nights" can be squeezed into the space of time between late Friday afternoon and early Sunday morning. The only way this can be done is to have a Wednesday or possibly a Thursday crucifixion.

For nearly two thousand years the church has observed Friday as the day of crucifixion. But is *tradition* the main reason for not giving up this observance? The clear evidence of the NT as well

as the specific meaning of that expression is clearly supportive of
a Friday crucifixion. Let us lay out the evidence and see if you
agree. The expression "three days and nights" only appears once
in the Matthew reference cited above. It is clear from the Gospels
that Jesus often prophesied that he would rise "on the third day"
(Matt 16:21; Mark 8:31; John 9:22). Simply put, that is the meaning
of "three days and three nights." In the Old Testament this exact
expression is used as equivalent to "the third day" (Gen 42:17, 18;
2 Chron 10:5, 12; Esther 4:16; 5:1; 1 Sam 30:12, 13). Contemporary
Jewish practice also supports the idea that "a portion of a day and
a night is as the whole of it" (Rabbi Eleazar ben Azariah *Babylonian Talmud, Avodah Zarah*, 5.11). For example, the Pharisees re-
called that Jesus predicted that he would rise "after three days" so
they asked that the tomb be guarded "until the third day" (Matt
27:63). The overwhelming evidence of the NT is that Jesus rose
"on the third day" (Matt 16:21; 17:23; 20:19; 27:64; Luke 9:22; 18:33;
24:7, 21, 46; Acts 10:40; 1 Cor 15:4). Therefore, "after three days"
must be equivalent to "on the third day" (Matt 27:63; Mark 8:31;
9:31).

The order was as follows. Jesus was laid in the tomb on the
"day of preparation," which is a technical expression for "Friday,"
because it is the day on which one prepares for the Sabbath on
the next day (Saturday; see, for example, Luke 23:54, 56). Even
down until modern times, the name for Friday in Greek is *par-
askeue*, literally "preparation day." If the crucifixion happened on
Wednesday or Thursday, then that would make either Thursday
or Friday the Sabbath, which is not the case. Rather, Luke tells us
that the very next day after "preparation day" was the Sabbath on
which the women rested. Then the next day, Sunday, the women
came to the tomb (Luke 24:1). Luke's order is clear: Preparation,
Sabbath, First Day. Later in that "first day" Cleopas and his friend
were walking to Emmaus and told the stranger who joined them

Figure 15: A nail through a heel bone from an ancient crucifixion. Exact replica, Israel Museum.

(Jesus) that it was the "third day" since Jesus was crucified: Friday=1, Saturday=2, Sunday=3. The evidence, therefore, is overwhelming that "three days and nights" is the same as "third day."

The Biblical evidence is clear that Jesus was crucified on a Friday. There are some additional logical problems with a Wednesday crucifixion, and it is these problems that are often overlooked. These will be my *fresh* ideas on this subject. The first problem is with the need to take "three days and three nights" literally as a seventy-two hour period. I hear them say dogmatically, "If the Bible says it, then it literally means 'three days and three nights.' Period." Proponents of this view, however, do not realize that they are proving too much by their insistence. If a literal seventy-two hours were meant, consider that Jesus was

placed in the tomb around four or five p.m. on Wednesday afternoon. Then he would have to be raised exactly seventy-two hours
later, at four to five p.m. on Saturday afternoon! But that raises a
very serious problem in that the Bible is very clear that Jesus was
not raised on Saturday afternoon, but early Sunday morning! So
proponents of a Wednesday crucifixion, by basing their argument on an overly-literal reading of Matthew 12:40, have ended
up with more problems than solutions.

The second logical problem with a Wednesday crucifixion is
so obvious that I am surprised it is not noticed more often. As a
matter of fact, I have only heard it from my seminary professor,
Gary Cohen, many years ago. Here it is. If Jesus was crucified and
buried quickly on Wednesday afternoon, the women would not
have waited until Sunday morning to anoint the body! They
would have come as soon as they could, namely on Friday morning, having rested on Thursday which was their supposed Sabbath in this theory. But the Gospels are clear that they came on
the first day of the week (Luke 24:1). In the Wednesday configu-
ration, that would have been too late because bodily decay and
smell would already have begun. This, in my opinion, is an insu-
perable problem for the Wednesday crucifixion advocates.

Some readers may become weary over the amount of time I
have spent on such a technical issue. I desire, therefore, to end
this chapter with some possibly fresh ideas on the burial of Jesus
in the nearby tomb of Joseph of Arimathea (Luke 23:50–53).
Many readers may not be aware that not only was Jesus' death
prophesied in the Old Testament Scriptures but also the manner
of his burial. To see this, we must give some brief attention to one
of the most amazing chapters prophesying the death of Jesus,
namely Isaiah 53.

In August of each year, the Jewish synagogue Scripture reading from the prophets is taken from the book of Isaiah. On one

Sabbath morning in August, the reading ends at Isaiah 52:12, just three verses before the end of that chapter. On the next Sabbath, the reading picks up at Isaiah 54:1. Thus, Isaiah 52:13 through 53:12 is omitted from the readings of the prophets in the synagogue. This table of Scripture readings has been well established since the early Middle Ages. Why is this section of Isaiah omitted from the synagogue readings? The typical answer from rabbis is that not every chapter of any prophet's book is chosen to be part of the readings. But such an answer simply is not sufficient. Why is this particular passage omitted, and why in such an obvious way is it skipped over? Could it be that the rabbis simply do not want to expose their synagogue attendees to the contents of this chapter? Why would they be afraid of it? We will address this issue again in the Epilogue.

This chapter speaks in the clearest and most detailed way of the Messiah of Israel, called the "servant," who is rejected by Israel but approved in God's plan as the means of salvation, atonement, and forgiveness for Israel and the whole world. According to Isaiah 52:14–15, the Lord's servant not only suffers for the people of Israel, but as a result of his suffering and death, his blood will "sprinkle many nations." Thus, this servant will be the Savior of the Gentiles as well. How have the Jewish rabbis viewed this passage? How it is quoted in the New Testament? And what is its relevance to our faith in Jesus as the Messiah and Savior?

In Acts 8, Philip led the Ethiopian eunuch to faith in Jesus through the words of this chapter. Philip responded to the eunuch's question, "About whom, I ask you, does the prophet say this, about himself or about someone else?" (Acts 8:34). Furthermore, I can't think of any other passage than Isaiah 53 that has been cited more by Jewish believers as the means God used to bring them to faith in Jesus.

This entire chapter is worthy of greater consideration, and we will do that in the Epilogue to this book. I now desire to focus on something that is often overlooked, even by Christians. Verse 9 includes a fascinating statement about his burial: "And they made his grave with the wicked and with a rich man in his death, although he had done no violence, and there was no deceit in his mouth." Even though he was sinless, he died with wicked men. But the verse says more than that. It literally says that his grave was appointed to be with wicked men, but he was with a rich man in his death. The word "wicked" in the first part of verse 9 is plural in the Hebrew (*reshaim*), but the word "rich" in the second part of the verse is singular in the Hebrew (*ashir*). Why the plural "wicked" but a singular "rich" man? A brief look at the Roman practice of crucifixion will help to answer that question.

Isaiah 53 and Psalm 22 are graphic prophetic descriptions of this method of execution that the Romans borrowed from the Carthaginians and then perfected to a gruesome art. People who were crucified were stripped of their clothes in shame and disgrace. Their hands and feet were pierced, and to hasten their death sometimes the side was pierced. The amazing thing is that in the time of Isaiah, as well as at the time when David wrote Psalm 22, crucifixion was not used as a method of execution among the Jewish people. It did not appear until hundreds of years later, adopted by the Romans from their Carthaginian enemies in the Punic Wars.

Jewish people have always been very concerned about burial. A body could not be left to die on a cross overnight and could not be buried with other people who were strangers. Reverent hands must take that body, wash it, anoint it, and bury it in a proper tomb. Victims of crucifixion, however, often did not have those privileges. Their bodies were most often cast into a common grave with other bandits and revolutionaries who had also been crucified. There was an exception to that practice in Jesus' case. Joseph of Arimathea, a secret believer in the Lord Jesus, interceded for the family and requested his body (Luke 23:50–53). Loving hands took the body of Jesus down from the cross, wrapped him, and put him into the tomb, thus fulfilling Isaiah 53:9. How else can we explain, but by the fulfillment of prophecy, this amazing statement that he was appointed to be with *wicked men* but that he was with a *rich man* when he died?*

*An excellent book about OT texts and the death of Christ is by David Allen, *According to the Scriptures: The Death of Christ in the Old Testament and the New* (SCM Press, 2019).

*See also John MacArthur, *The Gospel According to God: Rediscovering the Most Remarkable Chapter in the Old Testament* (Crossway, 2018).

Suggested prayer: "Lord Jesus, I do not pray before a crucifix, because I know that you did not stay on that cross. Help me to realize anew after reading a chapter like this that your suffering was programmed ahead of time by Isaiah. I need to also comprehend that you were even slain before the foundation of the world. May I join with the centurion in worship: 'Surely this man was the son of God.' I love you because you first love me."

Figure 16: These Jewish "Kokhim" tombs are very likely from the time of Christ, not very many feet from the most likely place of his burial.

11

DIFFERENT *VIEWPOINTS* OF THE RESURRECTION

I have heard and delivered dozens, perhaps hundreds, of sermons on the resurrection and a large number of people have mentioned the many evidences that Jesus rose bodily from the dead. Most of the evidences center on the significant number of eyewitnesses. Paul also mentioned the witnesses as the greatest evidence that took place (1 Cor 15:3–11). There is another evidence of the reality of Jesus' resurrection that I want to discuss in this chapter. Following this suggestion, I want to briefly discuss the order of Jesus' post resurrection appearances and how to sort out the greatest problem facing us in that regard, namely the claim that the reports seem to contradict each other. Finally, we will look again at Isaiah 53 and see that not only suffering and death but also victory and life were promised in that amazing chapter.

In 1982, there appeared a little volume with the simple title, *The Resurrection of Jesus*. It joined hundreds of books already available at that time on this subject. What was unique about the book was not even its argument, namely, that Jesus of Nazareth returned to life having clearly died. The uniqueness of the book was that the author was a Jew, and an Orthodox Jew as well!

Pinchas Lapide was a Jewish academic who actually specialized in New Testament history and writings. His book was not an attempt to explain away the resurrection of Jesus as a hoax or legend invented by his earliest followers. Here are his own words: "I accept the resurrection of Jesus not as an invention of the community of disciples, but as an historical event." When a leading orthodox Jew makes such a declaration, its significance can hardly be overstated.

As mentioned previously, Lapide was a rabbi and theologian who specialized in the study of the New Testament. In this book he convincingly shows that experience underlies the New Testament account of the resurrection, however much of the details of the narrative may be open to objection. He maintains that life after death is part of the Jewish faith experience, and he called attention to the resuscitations in the Hebrew Scriptures (see, for example, 2 Kings 4:32–37). The greatest evidence to Lapide that Jesus was seen alive by his followers was their changed lives, men who were transformed from fearful fleers to faithful followers and who endured, even to the point of dying for their faith. Lapide argued that we cannot explain away that something took place that radically transformed their attitudes and their lives. Simply stated, people do not die for what they know is a lie.

Now if you are hoping to hear about Lapide's baptism, I am sorry to inform you that he remained an Orthodox Jew until his death in 1997. While his book was a powerful argument that the greatest evidence of the resurrection of Jesus was the transformed lives of his followers, he did not believe that Jesus was Messiah, and that it is Jesus' messiahship, not his resurrection, which marks the division between Christianity and Judaism. Careful readers of the above will also take note that the resurrection of Jesus which Lapide championed is quite different from the resurrection of Jesus described in the New Testament. Like those in the Old Testament who returned to life, as well as Laza-rus and others in the New Testament who were raised (such as Jairus' daughter and Dorcas), these all eventually died. Jesus, however, rose again never to return to death! In other words, re-suscitation is not resurrection. That fact, however, should not limit the great value of Lapide's argument, namely that the trans-formed lives of the disciples, even the survival and existence of the Christian is the greatest evidence that he not only rose from the dead, but as we shall see, he also ascended to heaven in a glo-rified body.

There is another problem in the resurrection accounts, how-ever, and it is one we should not ignore. There are at least six books that recount Jesus' appearances after his resurrection – the four Gospels, Acts 1, and 1 Corinthians 15. If you compare those accounts some serious problems sometimes emerge with how to reconcile the apparent conflicts between them. How many women came to the tomb? One, two, or more? How many angels were there? One or two? In what order did Jesus appear to John and Peter and the rest of the disciples? The accounts are some-times difficult to reconcile. Now I believe that they *can* be recon-ciled and a good harmony of the Gospels attempts to do that. But why is it so hard? If they were recorded by eyewitnesses, why doesn't each of their accounts agree exactly on all the details? I want to suggest an answer to those questions and you may be surprised to learn that it comes from Hollywood!

Vantage Point was a 2008 political action thriller film that fo-cused on an assassination attempt on the President of the United States during a visit to Spain as seen from the various vantage points of the different characters. The film employed a storytell-ing technique through multiple perspectives. *Vantage Point* re-counts a series of events which are re-enacted from several dif-ferent viewpoints in order to reveal a truthful overall account of what happened. The film's technique can actually try the patience of viewers, since the account is reshot and retold a number of times from the different perspectives of those who witnessed the assassination. But what appear to be contradictions actually are the different perspectives of the viewers. It only happened once, but due to their different angles and perspectives, it looked like the accounts differed, although the event was obviously the same. Now I am not at all saying that the accounts of the resurrection are in conflict, but only that they may appear to be so because they are seen from the different perspectives of Mary Magdalene or Peter or John or Matthew or Paul. The various accounts in *Vantage Point* in the end did *not* contradict each other. They only appeared to do so because the witness did not see the entire picture and thus did not include everything he or she saw. In the same way, the Gospel writer simply did not include all the characters or details in his unique report.

We have looked at how the evidence of Jesus' resurrection is largely based on the eyewitness accounts of those who saw him and encountered him, even if they did not relate everything that they saw. There were approximately a dozen accounts of those who saw him, including the appearances to groups and also to Paul a few years afterward (Acts 9:1–19; 1 Cor 15). While we often talk about "the Great Commission," there are actually five forms of the Great Commission mentioned in the four Gospels and in Acts. Each one spoke slightly differently about the goal of the commission (Matt 28:18–20); the extent of the commission (Mark 16:15, if it was part of the original Mark); the message of the commission (Luke 24:46–47); the authority of the commission (John 20:21); and the strategy of the commission (Acts 1:8). These are not contradictory commissions but are complementary to each other.

In concluding this brief chapter of insights into the resurrection, I would like to return to that OT passage that I mentioned in the previous chapter on the crucifixion, Isaiah 53. Readers may be surprised to learn that this amazing chapter describes not only the death of the Messiah but describes also his return to life! Isaiah 53:10 says, "Yet it was the will of the LORD to crush him." Oftentimes we hear the question, "Did the Jews kill Jesus, or was it the Romans?" Actually, both were involved, but ultimately it was God's plan that his servant should suffer and die. "It was the will of the LORD to crush him; he has put him to grief." Later Peter would charge the Jewish leaders with blame but would carefully convey the balance, "This Jesus, delivered up according to the definite plan and foreknowledge of God, you crucified and killed by the hands of lawless men" (Acts 2:23). Returning to Isaiah 53, verse 10 adds, "When you will make his soul an offering for sin, he shall see his offspring; he shall prolong his days; and the will of the LORD shall prosper in his hand." Thus, his death would be an offering for sin, but after he became an offering for sin, the servant would "see his offspring and he will stretch out the length of his days" (literal translation).

There is a modern Jewish objection to this passage being used to apply to Jesus. "Isaiah 53 cannot be talking about Jesus," some Jews say, "because it says he will have many children and will live to be an old man. We know that Jesus died unmarried as a young man." But this verse does not teach that. When it says "he shall see his offspring (seed)," it is not describing his physical offspring. Rather, it is talking about his spiritual "seed." Psalm 22:30 affirms that "a posterity (offspring) will serve him." The word used in these passages is literally "seed" (*zera*). This word is used elsewhere in the Old Testament for "followers" (Zech 8:12; Mal 2:3). Also, "he shall prolong his days" does not mean that he will live a long life. It actually means that he will lengthen his days after he dies, since earlier in the verse he is actually described as dying. In other words, the subject of this verse was something that could have been expected by a close reader of Isaiah 53! This verse can only mean that the suffering servant will come back to life after he dies as a sin offering. So not only did Isaiah prophesy in this chapter about the Messiah's death, he also prophesied about his resurrection!

Verse 10 also speaks about the multitude of spiritual followers who will come to believe in him. As a matter of fact, that is also the meaning of verse 11: "Out of the anguish of his soul, he shall see and be satisfied." The ancient LXX translation says that "he will see light" and such a translation is supported by the complete ancient copy of Isaiah found among the Dead Sea scrolls. In other words, his death would not be a disappointment. There would be a purpose to his death, and he would be satisfied when he sees *life*, that is *life* after his death! The verse continues: "by his knowledge shall the righteous one, my servant, make many to be accounted righteous, and he shall bear their iniquities." When the Messiah comes and bears the iniquities of his people and then comes to life, many will believe in him and be justified, that is they will be declared as righteous. How will they be justified? By personally trusting him as their sin-bearer, Messiah, and Savior. Could any clearer presentation of the Gospel be written than this? And to think that it was written over seven hundred years before Jesus died and rose again in AD 30.*

▬▬▬▬▬▼▬▬▬▬▬

*One valuable source for the people and events of Passion Week is the reference work by Eckhard J. Schnabel, *Jesus in Jerusalem: The Last Days* (Eerdmans, 2018).

Suggested prayer: "Lord Jesus, not only your sacrificial death but also your glorious resurrection was foretold! You were not just a martyr, but you died and rose again for me and millions of my brothers and sisters! Am I part of the joy that was set before you that enabled you to endure your suffering, because you would then sit down with your Father in glory? I thank you so much that because you live I can live also."

Figure 17: A rolling-stone tomb from the first century.

12

HE'S GONE!
THERE HE IS!

I was nineteen years old, a sophomore in college, and preparing for the ministry. I was filled with zeal and was preparing to preach. We went out on an "extension" as it was called, and my ministry was preaching in prisons. I learned to preach in city and county jails and to chain gang prisoners. It was a Sunday and we were allowed into the large cell blocks. It was 1966 and segregation was still practiced at all levels in South Carolina, including separate facilities for white and black prisoners. After preaching to the white guys and usually receiving no interest at all from them, we went over to the black guys where many of them would put their feet on the floor and at least looked like they were listening. You see, these men, although serving time for crimes they had committed had often been raised by mommas who taught them to respect the Lord and his word. As I was waxing eloquent on Acts 1:9–11, I was going to work especially on verse 10: "And while they looked steadfastly toward heaven as he went up, behold, two men stood by them in white apparel." I will quote the King James Version because, what other version did we ever use in those days?

As I mentioned, my eloquence soon outstripped my accuracy as I expounded as follows. "And while Jesus was going up into heaven, two white men stood by them in apparel..." Before I could finish the sentence a sturdy fellow, sitting on his bunk with Bible in hand, interrupted me with the following, "Whoa preacher! It don't say two white men, it says two men in white clothes!" And suddenly, I was no longer a white man myself! I was a *red* man, embarrassed like a simple fool! I am not sure how or even if I ever recovered from that well-deserved interruption. I know, however, that I will never forget those "two men in white clothes" who spoke to the disciples who, with open mouth, were gazing into the sky that received the ascending Jesus from their sight.

I certainly recognize that the ascension of Jesus did not take place during what we call Passion Week, but forty days after the resurrection that took place on the eighth day of that special week. It is still appropriate that we take at least a glance at the event called the *ascension* as well as what we call his *session*, the arrival to the presence of his Father and his being seated at his right hand. What more can be said first about that event so graphically described by Luke in Acts 1:9–11. Those white clothed figures are not referred to as "angels" but as "men." That does not disqualify the idea that they were angels, but it does open up a possibility for us to at least consider their identity. These two men were with Jesus on the Mount of Olives and the only other time that Luke describes two men with Jesus on a mountain is in his Gospel in Luke 9:28–36. This event is referred to as "The Transfiguration." The other two Synoptists also describe the scene when Moses and Elijah appeared with Jesus in glory (Matt 17:1–8; Mark 9:2–8). Luke adds something, however, that is unique. He writes, "And behold, two men were talking with him, Moses and Elijah, who appeared in glory and spoke of his *departure*, which he was about to accomplish at Jerusalem" (Luke

Figure 18: Within the Church of the Holy Sepulcher stands the Edicule, over the likely site of Jesus' burial.

9:30–31). The word *departure* is *exodos* in the Greek, the word that is used as the title for the second book of the Pentateuch. It is interesting that these two OT worthies were talking about the Passion Week events that would climax not only in his death and his resurrection, but in his physical *departure* from this world, the event that we call the ascension. While I would not want to die on that hill (pardon the pun), I suggest that the two men in white clothes on the Mount of Olives were Moses and Elijah appearing with him at his departure. Luke's account mentions Jesus' white clothes at the Transfiguration (Luke 9:29), and we can probably conclude that the OT duo were also thus clothed. I have made some dogmatic suggestions for alternative readings in this book, and although I think it possible that Moses and Elijah were the two white-robed men, I recognize that these two in Acts 1:9–11 could also be angelic beings (see Luke 24:4, compared with Matt 28:2–3).

One of the most neglected doctrines in evangelical theology is the *ascension* along with its accompanying *session*, as some theologians call it. A survey of a prominent evangelical systematic theology reveals that it devotes twenty-one pages to Jesus' crucifixion, six pages to his resurrection and only one page to his ascension. It then devotes over thirty pages to the theological importance of the atonement, but only one page to the theological role of both the resurrection and ascension. Such an imbalance neglects the fact that Jesus' resurrection and ascension go together in the apostolic proclamation (Acts 2:24–36; 3:13). Not only Peter but also Paul affirmed, "Christ Jesus is the one who died—more than that, who was raised—who is at the right hand of God, who indeed is interceding for us" (Rom 8:34). Such neglect also is inconsistent with the earliest doctrinal statement of the early church, the Apostles' Creed. I will quote just part of that statement dating from its earliest form in the second century. Jesus "suffered under Pontius Pilate, was crucified, dead, and buried. The third day he rose again from the dead, he ascended into heaven, where he sits at the right hand of God the Father almighty, from whence he shall come to judge the living and the dead." While many scriptural texts could be cited about the importance of the ministry of the Lord Jesus in heaven, an entire book of the New Testament, the Letter to the Hebrews, is largely given over to the resurrection, ascension, and session ministry of Jesus Christ. Many Bible readers are surprised when they learn that the references to Jesus as our High Priest and his function as Priest are mentioned by those titles only in Hebrews.

As we have reminded ourselves in this little book about the role of the Old Testament in the Passion of our Lord, I remind you that the most quoted passage in the OT, Psalm 110, largely owes most of its citations to the Letter to the Hebrews. Our general neglect of the Book of Hebrews and of the role of Jesus' ascension and his heavenly session in evangelical theology have also led to a neglect of attention given to the heavenly work of our High Priest. Evangelicals rightly celebrate Good Friday and Resurrection Sunday, but we ignore Ascension Day, which was May 30 in the year 2019. Early Christians would be perplexed at our oversight.

Therefore, for my last fresh insight into Passion Week, I will briefly mention the nature of the atonement as it was finally accomplished in heaven by our High Priest, the ascended Lord Jesus. I will be brief but I hope it will lead us all to a fuller recognition that our Lord's accomplishment of redemption and atonement was found in its final fulfillment in heaven. In our previous discussion of Jesus' cry "It is finished" (John 19:30), I suggested that the reference there was to the finishing of the messianic prophecies about Jesus' suffering, such as Psalm 22 and Isaiah 53. It is my contention that atonement was begun on the cross and finished in heaven, because the Letter to the Hebrews teaches that very truth. Hebrews deals extensively with the sacrificial system in Leviticus, especially the sacrifices on the annual Day of Atonement. On the tenth day of the Jewish month Tishri (which falls in our October), the high priest killed an animal and placed its blood on the altar in the courtyard. Next he carried some of that blood into the Holy of Holies where he placed it on the *kapporet*, or the mercy seat as it is often translated. Only then was that sacrifice completed—not when the animal was killed, but when its blood was offered in the presence of the Holy One of Israel. "Then he shall kill the goat of the sin offering that is for the people and bring its blood inside the veil and do with its blood as he did with the blood of the bull, sprinkling it over the mercy seat and in front of the mercy seat. Thus *he shall make atonement* for the Holy Place, because of the uncleannesses of the people of Israel and because of their transgressions, all their sins" (Lev 16:15–16). See now Hebrews 9:11–12: "He (Christ) entered once for all into the holy places, not by means of the blood of goats and calves but by means of his own blood, *thus securing an eternal redemption.*" Evangelical scholar Donald Guthrie wrote: "The real effectiveness of the work of Christ is summed up in the words *thus securing an eternal redemption.* As here translated the participle 'securing' (*heuramenos*) is regarded as following from and subsequent to the entering. In this case the redemption is seen as the direct result of the offering" (*Tyndale NT Commentary*, 15, 189).

Hebrews 9:24 and 26 further teach that the second stage of Jesus' sacrifice took place upon his ascension and session before his Father. "For Christ has entered, not into holy places made with hands, which are copies of the true things, but into heaven itself, now to appear in the presence of God on our behalf.... as it is, he has appeared once for all at the end of the ages to put away sin by the sacrifice of himself." In the next chapter we also read, "But when Christ had offered for all time a single sacrifice for sins (in heaven), he sat down at the right hand of God (in heaven), waiting from that time until his enemies should be made a footstool for his feet" (Heb 10:12–13). It is there in the heavenly Holy of Holies that as both priest and sacrifice he secured our eternal redemption. And it is there where he intercedes for us and receives our prayers as our heavenly High Priest (Heb 4:14–16).*

Nothing I have written should meet with any disagreement on the part of Bible believers. Recognizing that our atonement was finally completed in heaven will not diminish our appreciation of the cross work of our Savior. It will only expand our appreciation for his finishing that atoning work by offering himself to the Father and then sitting down at the right hand of the Father (Heb 10:12). This truth has very practical consequences for believers as Hebrews 4:14–16 says. It is there at that heavenly throne of grace where sinning believers find both mercy and grace – mercy for our past sins and failures and grace to help us to be holy and successful in our daily walk.

That is the final reason why I am so passionate about the Passion Week!

*For a scholarly defense of the above approach to Jesus' offering himself in heaven see R. B. Jamieson, *Jesus' Death and Heavenly Offering in Hebrews* (Cambridge University Press, 2019); and David M. Moffitt, "Blood, Life, and Atonement: Reassessing Hebrews' Christological Appropriation of Yom Kippur" in *The Day of Atonement: Its Interpretations in Early Jewish and Christian Traditions*, eds. Thomas Hieke and Tobias Nicklas (Brill, 2011).

Suggested prayer: "Lord Jesus, we rightly talk about your death and your resurrection, but how rarely do we talk about your sitting down with the Father! We often talk about what you did and also what you will do, but we think little about what you are doing now! I come boldly to your present throne of grace, because I so need your mercy for my past sins and your grace to help me in my struggle against future sins. Your grace is sufficient."

Figure 19: The resurrected Jesus met his disciples in Galilee, also the region of much of his ministry, where he no doubt saw many such sunrises (Mark 1:35).

EPILOGUE

_____

PROPHECY AND THE PASSION

"Throughout the four Passion narratives there is a con-
certed effort to show that the shocking things that
happened during the last week of Jesus' life, including his death on the cross, were foretold in Scripture and all along
part of God's plan. *Nothing* in that last week happened by acci-
dent or against the will of God is the message of the Evangelists,
not even Jesus' death on the cross" (Ben Witherington, *Biblical
Theology: The Convergence of the Canon* [Cambridge University
Press, 2019], 270).

At various points in this little volume, we have tried to point
out how such OT texts as Psalms 22 and 110, as well as Daniel 7
and Zechariah 9 and 12 were "fulfilled" in the events of the death
of Jesus. We have also mentioned more than a few times the role
of Isaiah 53 in this drama. Even at the risk of repeating some
things that I have already written, I would like to revisit in more
detail the fourth of Isaiah's "Servant Songs" in Isaiah 52:13–53:12. I
do this to solidify in the readers' minds that the Passion was actually programmed and was not just a tragedy that befell a Galilean
itinerant whose "Passover Plot" failed and blew up in his face.

As I wrote in a previous chapter, on a Sabbath morning in August, the *Haftarah* reading from the Prophets in the synagogue
ends at Isaiah 52:12. On the next Sabbath the reading picks up at

Isaiah 54:1. Isaiah 52:13 through 53:12 is simply omitted. Thus this important passage is never read in the synagogue as part of the assigned Scripture readings.

The typical answer from rabbis why it is omitted is that not every chapter of any prophet's book is chosen to be part of the readings. The vital question is why it is it skipped over? Could it be that the rabbis simply do not want to expose their synagogue attendees to the contents of this chapter?

This passage in Isaiah speaks in the clearest and most detailed way of the Messiah of Israel, called the "servant," who is rejected by Israel but approved in God's plan as the means of salvation, atonement, and forgiveness for Israel and the whole world. In the "prologue" of the song, the Lord's servant not only suffers for the people of Israel, but as a result of his suffering and death, his blood will "sprinkle many nations" (Isa 52:14–15). This servant for Israel will also be the Savior of the Gentiles. Isaiah 53 is such an important passage that we must look at it closer in light of its role in Jewish tradition. How have the Jewish rabbis viewed this passage? How it is quoted in the New Testament? And what is its relevance to a faith in Jesus as the Messiah and Savior?

God has used Isaiah 53 in amazing ways in history, beginning in Acts 8, where Philip led the Ethiopian eunuch to faith in Jesus through the words of this chapter. Philip responded to the eunuch's question: "About whom, I ask you, does the prophet say this, about himself or about someone else?" (Acts 8:34) by explaining to him that Isaiah was speaking about Jesus. Furthermore, Isaiah 53 has been cited by Jewish believers more than any text as the means God used to bring them to faith in Messiah Jesus.

The twelve verses of this chapter are divided into four distinct sections of three verses each. In Isaiah 53:1–3, we first see the servant's *submission*; then in verses 4–6, the servant's *substitution*; then in verses 7–9, the servant's *sinlessness*; and in verses

10–12, the triumphant ending of this chapter, the servant's *satisfaction*.

"Who has believed what they heard from us?" Isaiah asks. In other words, not many people will accept this message. "And to whom has the arm of the LORD been revealed?" (v. 1). It will take a revelation from the Lord for people to understand this message of the suffering servant. Verse 2 says, "For he grew up before him like a young plant, and like a root out of dry ground; he had no form nor majesty that we should look at him, and no beauty that we should desire him." This speaks of the lowly beginnings of the servant. Miriam and Joseph were humble people from a small town who had to bring the poor person's offering when they presented Jesus at the Temple (Luke 2:22–24).

Isaiah 53:2 says that when he would come forth, he would display "no beauty that we should desire him." There was nothing in the appearance of the Galilean peasant that attracted people. While this does not imply ugliness, it does mean that his visible appearance was not what commended him to people. On the contrary, they would reject him: "He was despised and rejected by men; a man of sorrows, and acquainted with grief; and as one from whom men hide their faces he was despised, and we esteemed him not" (v. 3). He did not draw the admiration of the religious leaders of his day. They often despised him. When he spoke, however, it was with power and authority, and the common people marveled at the gracious words that came forth from his mouth (Luke 4:22).

Verses 4–6 then tell of the servant's **substitution** in the behalf of others:

Surely he has borne our griefs and carried our sorrows; yet we esteemed him stricken, smitten by God, and afflicted. But he was wounded for our transgressions; he was crushed for our iniquities; upon him was the chastisement that brought us peace, and with his stripes we are healed. All we like sheep have gone astray; we have turned every one to his own way; and the LORD has laid on him the iniquity of us all.

He did not suffer because of anything he did nor because he was a martyr. He suffered for others. Over and over the words "our" and "us" are used here, indicating that he suffered not for his own sins but for the sins of others; he died in the place of other people, bearing their transgressions.

In this regard, it is important to examine the matter of what the rabbis say about Isaiah 53. Prior to about AD 1100, even the rabbis acknowledged that Isaiah 53 must apply to the Messiah. For example, the *Targum Jonathan*, written in the second century AD, says of Isaiah 52:13: "Behold my servant, the Messiah, shall prosper." The rabbis of the Talmudic period always referred to the servant as the Messiah, even though they did not apply it to Jesus. A contemporary Jewish scholar, Daniel Boyarin in his book *The Jewish Gospels* acknowledges that the ancient Jewish interpretation of Isaiah 53 was that the servant was the Messiah.

Around AD 1100, however, a great teacher named Rashi (Rabbi Shlomo Itzaki) inaugurated a new interpretation of Isaiah 53 that today has become the general Jewish interpretation of this passage. Rashi said that Isaiah 53 does not refer to Jesus, nor does it even refer to the Jewish Messiah. Rather, it refers to Israel as a nation, who have been despised and rejected by the Gentiles and have suffered at their hands. Rashi pointed to other passages in Isaiah where the term "servant" does indeed appear to refer to Israel as a people (e.g., 44:1).

How do we respond to that explanation in light of Isaiah 53:4–6? First, while there are some passages in the Book of Isaiah where the term "servant" does apply to Israel, there are other passages where it simply cannot refer to Israel. For example, consider Isaiah 49:6, "It is too light a thing that you should be my servant to raise up the tribes of Jacob and to bring back the preserved of Israel; I will make you as a light for the nations, that my salvation may reach to the end of the earth." In other words, the servant is not identified as Israel in this verse, but as an individual who will bring Israel back to God.

Israel as a nation was called to be a light; they were called to be righteous, but Isaiah clearly stated that they were unrighteous. There would be one who would come, however, called the servant, who would be the ideal Israel and would be successful where the people failed. God appointed this ideal person, this ideal Israel, to be his servant to bring Israel back to the Lord. That is why in Isaiah the word "servant" can sometimes be the people and sometimes an individual within the people who is their Messiah. Scholars refer to this characteristic as "corporate solidarity."

There is a clear indication that God's servant is a person, as indicated by the pronouns used: "Surely he has borne *our* griefs and carried *our* sorrows; yet *we* esteemed him stricken, smitten by God, and afflicted" (v. 4). The singular personal pronouns cannot refer to Israel because that people are referred to by the plural words *we* and *our*. The singular pronouns must refer to an individual. Israel cannot die for Israel, but this individual will die for Israel as their representative.

Furthermore, the servant is righteous: "The righteous one, my servant, will make many to be righteous" (v. 11). The servant was to be sinless. This certainly has never been true of Israel, for Isaiah himself declared how sinful Israel was (see, for example, Isa 1:4–6). Therefore, the submissive servant cannot be Israel. The servant also suffers voluntarily and silently: "He was oppressed and he was afflicted, yet he opened not his mouth" (v. 7). Israel never suffered in this way. There were a number of instances, even during the awful experiences of the Holocaust, when Jews rebelled. They formed underground resistance groups and fought against the Nazis with what strength and weapons they had. They may have suffered in secret but not in silence.

Finally, the servant dies: "Yet it was the will of the LORD to crush him; he has put him to grief; when his soul makes an offering for sin..." (v. 10). Israel has never died but has continued to live despite her suffering. Therefore, the chapter's *servant* cannot speak of Israel, but the language must describe an individual who will die in the place of Israel. As verse 6 states, "All we like sheep have gone astray; we have turned every one to his own way, and the LORD has laid on him the iniquity of us all." The servant died the death of a substitute to atone for the sins of Israel.

In verses 7–9 we see the servant's **sinlessness**. "He was oppressed, and he was afflicted, yet he opened not his mouth; like a lamb that is lead to the slaughter, and like a sheep that before its shearers is silent, so he opened not his mouth" (v. 7). This is exactly what happened in the trial of Jesus when false witnesses were bribed to bring false charges against him. He did not speak in his own defense. He did not object to the unjust treatment. He did not strike back at the abuse, but willingly accepted it. The silence of Jesus at his trial was the graphic fulfillment of Isa 53:7.

Verse 8 adds, "By oppression and judgment he was taken away; and as for his generation, who considered that he was cut off out of the land of the living; stricken for the transgression of my people?" "My people" clearly refers to Israel, while the servant dies for the transgression of Israel. He was cut off out of the land of the living—a clear reference to his death. Therefore, this cannot be Israel. Israel was not cut off from the land of the living but is still very much in existence today. According to the promises of God, this individual would die as a sinless sacrifice for others.

"And they made his grave with the wicked and with a rich man in his death, although he had done no violence, and there was no deceit in his mouth" (53:9). Even though he was sinless, he died with wicked men. The verse says that his grave was appointed to be with wicked *men*, but he was with a rich *man* in his death. The word "rich" in the second part of the verse is singular in the Hebrew (*ashir*). Why the plural "wicked" but a singular "rich" man?

Jewish custom did not permit a body to be left on a cross overnight and it could not be buried with strangers, but washed, anointed, and buried it in a proper tomb. Crucifixion victims were usually cast into a common grave with the other crucified criminals. Joseph of Arimathea, however, requested his body (Luke 23:50–53), and loving hands wrapped him and placed him into the tomb, thus fulfilling Isaiah 53:9. Thus Jesus was appointed to be with wicked men but he was with a rich man after he died!

Finally, in verses 10–12 we read of the servant's **satisfaction**. Verse 10 says, "Yet it was the will of the LORD to crush him." Often we hear the following question: "Did the Jews kill Jesus, or was it the Romans?" Actually, both were involved, but ultimately it was God's plan that his servant suffer. "It was the will of the LORD to crush him; he has put him to grief. When you will make his soul an offering for sin, he shall see his offspring; he shall prolong his days; the will of the LORD shall prosper in his hand" (v. 10). Thus, his death would be an offering for sin. And after he became an offering for sin, the servant would "see his offspring and he will stretch out longer the length of his days" (literal translation).

There is a modern Jewish objection to this passage being used to apply to Jesus. "Isaiah 53 cannot be talking about Jesus," some Jews say, "because it says he will have many children and will live to be an old man. We know that Jesus died unmarried as a young man." But this verse does not teach that. When it says "he shall see his offspring," it is not describing his physical seed, but is describing his spiritual seed. Psalm 22:30 says, "Posterity (off-spring) shall serve him." The word used in these passages is literally "seed" (*zera*). This word is used elsewhere in the Old Testament for "followers" (Zech 8:12; Mal 2:3). Also, "he shall prolong his days" does not mean that he will live a long life. It actually means that he will lengthen his days *after* he dies, since earlier in the verse he is described as dying. This can only mean that he will come back to life after he dies as a sin offering. So not only did Isaiah prophesy in this chapter about the Messiah's death; he also prophesied about his resurrection!

Verse 10 speaks about the multitude of spiritual followers who will come to believe in him. That is also the meaning of verse 11: "Out of the anguish of his soul, he shall see and be satisfied." The ancient Greek translation of the Old Testament, known as the Septuagint, includes the noun "light" after "he shall see." The great Isaiah scroll, one of the famous Dead Sea Scrolls, dating to before the time of Messiah Jesus, also clearly says, "He will see light." In other words, after his death he will see the light of life! This can only mean that he will see life after his death.

Furthermore, there would be no disappointment in his death, but rather he would be satisfied: "by his knowledge shall the righteous one, my servant, make many to be accounted righteous, and he shall bear their iniquities." Isaiah declared that when the Messiah comes and bears the iniquities of his people, many will believe in him and be justified, i.e., they will be declared as righteous. How will they be justified? By personally trusting him as their sin-bearer, Messiah, and Savior. Could any clearer presentation of the Gospel be written than this? And to think that it was written over seven hundred years before Jesus died and rose again in AD 30.

This amazing chapter ends with the words, "Therefore I will divide him a portion with the many, and he shall divide the spoil with the strong, because he poured out his soul to death and was numbered with the transgressors; yet he bore the sin of many, and makes intercession for the transgressors" (v. 12). This verse is a summary statement of all that has happened to the Messiah in this chapter. He was numbered with transgressors, bearing the sin of many and pouring out his soul unto death. But he also has a reward—dividing a portion with the great and dividing the spoil with the strong. The Messiah will not be disappointed in the end—he will be satisfied. He will be rewarded for his suffering and death by seeing a multitude come to know him and thus he will make intercession for the transgressors. Many have seen a New Testament restatement of Isaiah 53:12 in the words of Hebrews 12:2: "Looking to Jesus, the founder and perfecter of our faith, who for the joy that was set before him endured the cross, despising the shame, and is seated at the right hand of the throne of God."

For nearly two millennia multitudes of Jewish people and Gentiles have come to know the Lord's lasting forgiveness through discovering the suffering Messiah in this chapter. They have trusted Jesus of Nazareth as their sin-bearer, the one who fulfilled in his life and ministry the prophecies about the suffering servant in Isaiah 53. Perhaps the rabbis don't want their people to come to the same conclusion that these Jews have—that Isaiah 53 prophesied about a suffering Messiah, and that Jesus fulfilled that prophecy in dozens of amazing ways.

Surviving the Holocaust, Rabbi Sam Stern met some young believers in America who shared the good news of the Messiah with him. He was unconvinced until a friend asked him to read the words of Isaiah 53 which he had typed on a piece of paper with no chapter or verse numbers. When asked what he was reading, Sam replied that it was some writing by a Christian about Jesus' death! When told that it was written by a Jewish prophet named Isaiah, he was provoked to look in his Hebrew Bible and found that it was the same as the English he had read.

Sam Stern pointed to that experience as the time when he began to seriously consider the message that Jesus was the Messiah. Sam faithfully ministered the good news about the Messiah in Brooklyn until his death in the early 1980s. Like Sam, thousands of Jewish people from New Testament days until today have pointed to Isaiah 53 as the one passage more than any other that opened their hearts to the message that Jesus is the Messiah of Israel.

That is why am I so "Passionate about Passion Week!" The message of Messiah Jesus' death, resurrection, and ascension has given me new life. This message can do the same for you, whether you are a Gentile or Jew, as you trust him as your personal sin-bearer who died and regained life to save you from death and give you new life!*

———————▼———————

*For further study of Isaiah 53 and every other prophecy about the Messiah, see the *Moody Handbook of Messianic Prophecy: Studies and Expositions of the Messiah in the Old Testament*, eds. Michael Rydelnik and Edwin Blum (Moody Publishers, 2019). I was privileged to write the chapter on Noah's Blessing on Shem from Gen 9:25–27.

Prayer of the Author: "Lord Jesus, I have told my readers that I am passionate about your passion week. May this be more than a clever book title. Your grace to me meant that you became poor so I can become rich. I am so rich in treasures that can never be lost. I am such a blest man, Lord. 'May the God of peace who brought again from the dead our Lord Jesus, the great shepherd of the sheep, make us perfect in every good work to do his will, working in us that which is pleasing in his sight, to whom be glory forever. Amen'" (Heb 13:20–21).

CPSIA information can be obtained
at www.ICGtesting.com
Printed in the USA
BVHW090233030321
601506BV00006B/115